Light on

AṢṬĀṄGA YOGA

B.K.S. Iyengar

ALCHEMY

First Published in 2008 by

ALCHEMY

ALCHEMY PUBLISHERS
4767/23, Pratap Street, Daryaganj
New Delhi - 110002

Distributed by :-

Mehras Books Pvt. Ltd.

15, Bankim Chatterjee Street
2nd Floor, Kolkata - 700 073

4767/23, Pratap Street, Daryaganj
New Delhi - 110 002

G 1 & 2, Ghaswalla Towers,
PG Solanki Path, Off Lamington Road,
Mumbai - 400 007

New India Book Source
5/1 Sirur Park Road, Thanappa Mansion, Seshadripuram
Bangalore -560020

Rupa & Co. (Allahabad)
135, South Malaka, Allahabad - 211001

ISBN 10: 81-8046-051-7
ISBN 13: 978-81-8046-051-7

Cover design: Nilesh Walawalkar

Printed and bound in India by
M/s. Decora Printers, Mumbai

ॐ

|| *Sri Gurubhyoḥ Namaḥ* ||

|| *Gurur brahmā gurur viṣṇu gurur devo maheśvaraḥ*
guru sākṣāt parabrahma tasmai 'srī gurave namaḥ ||

|| *Ṣa eṣaḥ pūrveṣām api guruḥ kālena anavacchedāt* ||

GOD
is the first,
foremost and absolute Guru,
unconditioned by time.

Yoga is equaminity
Yoga is skillfulness in action
Yoga is restraint of the sorrows of *citta*

An Offer to the Lovers of Yoga

INTRODUCTION

In 1996, I gave a talk on Light on *Aṣṭāṅga Yoga* at the Ramāmaṇi Iyengar Memorial Yoga Institute and YOG published this in 1999 for the benefit of the students of the Institute.

At present, Alchemy publishers of New Delhi have taken the rights to publish it and I am delighted to offer this treatise on *Aṣṭāṅga Yoga* through my publishers so that it not only benefits its practitioners but also those who are un-acquainted with the subject to get an overall view of this yogic philosophy that is hidden in the yogic texts.

As it was first published verbaṭim, I thought that I should re-read the original, revise and edit so that the readers grasp the subject with an un-interrupted flow of attention.

In order to understand the importance of yoga and its values, man needs to have a good background regarding the origin of the Universe (macrocosm) and the world and their relationship with man (microcosm) and God. Without this essential background of the science of cosmology, it may become difficult to understand the structure and the constitution of man and the role that yoga plays in uniting the macrocosm *(brahmāṇḍa)* with the microcosm *(piṇḍāṇḍa)* as human being is regarded as the representation in miniature form of the universe.

According to *sāṁkhya darśana* (philosophy), God is the seed of the universe and knowledge. He created *puruṣa,* the soul and *prakṛti,* the nature with its twenty-four principles. These principles of nature mould and blend with its three *guṇa-s* or qualities, namely, *sattva* (illumination), *rajas* (vibration or motion) and *tamas* (inertia or laziness). (See table one in the text.)

The hub of man's life is interdependent upon these *guṇa-s* wherein all the twenty-four principles of nature of man revolve around them. Here *aṣṭāṅga yoga* comes handy in order to put an end to this revolving wheel of nature.

Upaniṣad-s say *saṁyoga yoga ityukto jivātma paramātmanaḥ II.* It means that yoga is the union of the individual soul with the Universal Soul. Yoga acts as an instrument in associating *(saṁyoga),* nature *(prakṛti)* with the Soul or the Self *(puruṣa)* in order to bring this union. Hence this union *(saṁyoga)* of nature with God is called yoga.

As *Light on Aṣṭāṅga Yoga* explains this union through the perfection in *āsana-s* and *prāṇāyāma-s* along with the principles of *yama* and *niyama* which help to eradicate the divisions and differences between body and mind, and mind and Self, so that the *sādhaka* or the practitioner becomes only a seer and lives in a state of firmness and serenity forever. *tataḥ dvandvāḥ anabhighātaḥ II"* (*Y.S.,* II.48).

The dualities between body *(prakṛti)* and Soul *(puruṣa)* ceases in this precise state of *sādhanā* making the *sādhaka* to live in a state of beatitude as he has built up the union between the intelligence of the consciousness that sprouts from nature to that of the shining intelligence of the Soul. *"sattva puruṣayoḥ śuddhi sāmye kaivalyam iti II"* (*Y.S.*, III.56).

This is the real health, real awareness and freedom from all bondage. From then on he ceases to do or act, that causes no pains, sorrows and afflictions on himself or on mankind. *"tataḥ kleśa karma nivṛttiḥ II"* (*Y.S.*, IV.30).

According to the *yoga sūtra-s* of Patañjali, the subject is divided and discussed in two parts. The first part deals with the principles of the *Aṣṭāṅga Yoga* and the second part explains its application in the daily practices.

I have tried my best in unfolding the subtle parts of yoga so that the readers savour the flavour of yoga like seeing and enjoying the blooming petals of the flowers from a healthy tree. At the same time, the subject matter carries sub-titles so that one can refer and re-refer according to the topic of interest and need. Also I have included the tables and illustrations of the *āsana-s* as well as the *sūtra-s* which are referred in the text.

I feel that this book is special and unique, defining lucidly the *vṛtti-s, kleśa-s* and *antarāya-s* at various levels with fresh ideas for readers to grasp and reach the finest state of the consciousness.

I am indebted to Alchemy Publishers in presenting this work to larger readers with new thoughts on yoga which may possibly ignite their zeal further in their *sādhanā*.

B. K. S. IYENGAR

CONTENTS

Chapter 1: Exposition of Principles

Chapter 2: Application of Principles

ILLUSTRATIONS

Table No.

Chapter 1:

Exposition of Principles

THE NEED OF MANKIND

Yoga is as old as civilisation. *Brahmā*, the creator of the world, created yoga and therefore the world and yoga came into existence together. It has been known to yogi-s since time immemorial. The *vaidika* text *Pāñcharātra* declares,

Hiraṇya garbha yogasya proktā nānyaḥ purātanaḥ II

Brahmā, the creator, is the founder of yoga. Yoga is a divine subject given by a divine being, the creator himself. It is very interesting to see how yoga was visualised by our ancestoral *sādhaka-s*, and practitioners.

The word yoga is derived from the *Sanskṛt* root-word *'yujir'*, meaning to bind, join, attach and yoke. Yoga means to concentrate one's attention or direct one's energy in search of the Ultimate Truth. It also means union or communion, the true union of one's will with the will of God. Yoga is a complete science having the firm foundation of philosophy and art.

Each science has a clear and a distinct definition, classifying its scope, aims and utilities. In the same way yoga too has its own definition, its scope, its subject matter and aim. But all these things happen as science if the *sādhaka* has touched and reached the fullness in his development in yogic *sādhanā*. No definition on any subject or science can be pre-decided or pre-determined. Chemistry was not defined right at its beginning when it was first discovered. As the picture of chemistry began to get refined by scientists, they were able to give a definition of chemistry. Now, we read chemistry and are able to arrive at its definition immediately. We do this because what had been unknown is made known. But when we see the full history of science, we realise how long it took for that unknown to become known.

Yoga has not been an exception. Lord Brahmā certainly did not hand over to human beings a fully refined, complete yogic science, straight away. It was discovered by the *ṛṣi-s,* the *muni-s* and *yogi-s* in order to find out the truth. Though it was *Brahmā's* creation, it was the yogi-s' discovery. Lord *Brahmā* created everything, but left it to mankind to search and research, to discover and rediscover, to invent and reinvent in order to find the subtlest and finest points in yoga.

Man is full of desires, hopes, temptations and attachments. Our ancestors realised that these desires and attachments are never-ending. The more one tries to fulfil and satisfy the desires, the more momentum they gather, until they become like a huge tidal wave. The ocean's waves make the sand wet and at the same time they have the potential to draw man completely under, or even to wash away the cities. The *ṛṣi-s, muni-s* and *yogi-s,* being very sensitive, could see people getting drawn into the great ocean of desire – *vāsanā.* They could see the need for freedom from desires. They felt the need for a solution, for a light, which could save lives from being drawn into the ocean of desires. They realised that if one can get drawn or pulled into the ocean of desires, there must be a way in saving one from getting drawn in or to be pulled out.

THE DEFINITIONS OF YOGA

It was with this need to save human beings from the ocean of desires that yoga was discovered and its light of knowledge uncovered. They did not find its varying definitions at first. These came later after the subject matter was discovered with persistent practices and scrutinizing each experience with certain methodologies. Therefore, we have to look back over its history to trace yoga's origins and definitions.

Some of the early definitions can be found in the *Veda-s*, *Upaniṣad-s*, *Āraṇyaka-s*, *Saṁhitā-s* and *Yoga Sūtra-s* as well as in the *Mahābhārata* and *Bhagavad Gītā*. When we see these definitions and reflect on them, we realise how the definitions of yoga changed in accordance with the needs of the society of those times and the ways as understood by the *sādhaka-s*. As the needs changed, the capacity of man's discriminative intelligence changed and the definition also changed. Let us look at these changes.

The *Ahirbudhnya Saṁhitā* gives a clear and complete definition of yoga,

Saṁyoga yoga ityukto jivātma paramātmanaḥ II

It explains that yoga is the union between the individual soul and the Universal Soul.

At the time of the *veda-s* and *saṁhitā-s* the intelligence of human beings had reached a culmination point. Man's needs at that time were also less and greed was rare. The *sādhaka-s* were mature, their religiosity in *sādhanā* was strong, hence, they could think at the level of the soul. Therefore, in the *Ahirbudhnya Saṁhitā,* we read that yoga is a union between *jīvātman* – the individual soul – and *paramātman* – the Universal Soul. In fact, the *Ahirbudhnya Saṁhitā* has its origin in *Pāñcarātra* – *pāñca* = five, *rātra* = nights. It is said that Lord Nārāyaṇa taught spiritual knowledge as well as Yoga to *nitya sūri-s* – eternal souls, for five days and five nights, hence the word *'Pāñcarātra'.*

Later, in the *Bhagavad Gītā,* Lord Krishna realised that the intellectual capacity of the yoga practitioner, the *sādhaka,* had lessened from what it had been at the time of the *Veda-s.* Naturally, He had to soften the path and make it understandable. Lord Krishna, showing His 'mother's heart' towards His devotees, defined yoga on two levels: *jñāna* and *karma* – knowledge and action. He defined,

Samattvam yoga ucchyate II" -- Equanimity is yoga

and

Yogaḥ karma-su kauśalam II – Yoga is skillfulness in action.

Let us look at the first explanation on yoga from *Gita*: "Equanimity is yoga". This equanimity is not just external, to show off. This equanimity has to come from within, from the heart – the core and one's being. There should be a thorough understanding between the intelligence of the soul and the intelligence of the consciousness. The soul with all its vehicles, namely *citta* – consciousness, *karmendriya-s* – organs of action, *jñānendriya-s* – senses of perception, *ahaṁkāra* – ego, *buddhi* – intelligence and *manas* – mind, have to be unified and integrated so that one realises the pureness of the soul. When one realises this pure soul, then one knows that the soul in everyone is the same and consequently one treats each and everyone with equanimity. The practitioner who is a *jñāni*, experiences this sense of equanimity.

Now, let me take you to look at the second explanation of the same text: "Yoga is skillfulness in action. What is a skillful action? It is an action that is performed with skillful intelligence. Each action yields fruit. One cannot perform any action purposelessly without there being some fruits or results. No one does action without expecting or receiving its fruit. Lord Krishna is not saying to do the action aimlessly. He is saying that it is the selfish motive behind the action that one has to avoid. The moment selfishness interferes, the action gets tainted. If a good purpose behind the action vanishes, then the work undertaken and scope for action gets distorted. So Lord Krishna says that one should not expect or accept any reward or fruit of his actions. The action undoubtedly ends with fruits. Listen to what Krishna says to Arjuna that if you are slain in the battle, you go to heaven and if victorious, you enjoy the soverignity of the earth. Therefore, stand up and resolve to fight as the effort in either way is glorious.

hato vā prāpsyasi svargaṁ jitvā vā bhokṣyase mahīm

tasmād uttiṣṭha kaunteya yuddhāya kṛta-niścayaḥ // (B.G; *II.37)*

Our responsibility is to remove the 'selfish' aspect in our action. Then we realise that, that action becomes skillful and vast in its scope.

It is impossible to do any action without an aim, but it is possible to do it without ambition. Aim and ambition are not the same. Aim must be for the universal good, for universal use and utility, but ambition always has a selfish motive and a selfish end. The desires – *vāsanā-s* – are eternal in us. Ambitions are the sprouts of *vāsanā*. It is the *vāsanā-s* that lead us to work with ambition. Work done with ambition is *sakāma karma*. Work that is performed abandoning the fruits of action or done desirelessly and dispassionately, without a tinge of selfishness is *niṣkāma karma*. Lord Krishna prefaced His teaching by explaining that *'niṣkāma karma'* is action without the expectation of fruits. He recommends *kauśala karma* or skillful action to feel what *niṣkāma karma* is.

The word *kauśala* or *kauśalam* has its projection in *abhyāsa* and *vairāgya* (see Table – 13). *Abhyāsa* means just practice and *vairāgya* means desireless practice. The action or *karma* indicates *abhyāsa*. Lord Krishna is not discarding *karma*. He wants everyone to do *karma* and that is *abhyāsa*. However, the *abhyāsa* has to be done with *vairāgya*. *Vairāgya* is hidden in the word *kauśalam*. Lord Krishna does not want *vairāgya* to be expressed or exhibited; He wants the *sādhaka* to do his *karma* with skillful application of consciousness so that the action is untainted by the ego, the intelligence and the mind. He says, "Let not the mind hanker after the fruits. Let not the intelligence calculate the gains. Let not the ego take pride in success or gain".

The *Ahirbudhnya Saṁhitā* defines yoga in terms of devotion - *bhakti*. Being *saṁyoga yoga*, it is advocated as the union between the individual soul and the Universal Soul. The *Bhagavad Gītā* defines yoga as, equanimity and skillfulness in action

Now, let us see how Patañjali defines yoga. In his time, he had to change the definition to codify the subject of yoga, not only with scientific analysis but also with precise, practical means. Perhaps he was able to see the lack of understanding and ignorance in people regarding the soul. He made a distinction between *citta* and *cit*. He defines *Citta* as consciousness and *cit* as soul. A common man treats *cit* the soul and *citta* consciousness, as one. However, without disciplining the consciousness – the *citta*, the *cit* – the soul cannot be distinguished from the *citta*. So, Patañjali defines yoga at two levels. Firstly, at a disciplined level as *yoga anuśāsanaṃ* – yoga as a discipline and secondly as *citta vṛtti nirodha* – restraint of mental fluctuations and modifications.

The entire yogic philosophy of Patañjali begins with these two *sūtra-s,*

Atha yogānuśāsanam ll" and *Yogaḥ citta vṛtti nirodhaḥ ll"*

Firstly it insists the discipline and finally the restraint on yourself.

Yogic philosophy is a practical philosophy. It is not a matter to be described, discussed or debated. It is a subject to be experienced. If we read these first two *sūtra-s* with careful attention, we see that *abhyāsa* and *vairāgya* are hidden in them. *"Atha yogānuśāsanam ll",* means the discipline of yoga and *"Yogaḥ citta vṛtti nirodhaḥ ll",* means the cessation, or restraint, or renunciation of the movements of consciousness. The former indicates *abhyāsa* – practice – and the latter indicates *vairāgya* – renunciation or dispassion.

Yoga philosophy is purely a practical subject which revolves around *abhyāsa* and *vairāgya.* If *abhyāsa* is the positive current of the consciousness, then *vairāgya* is its negative current. Patañjali blends *abhyāsa* and *vairāgya* in a very practical way.

In the modern age we have to look at this practical subject from a different angle. *Abhyāsa* – practice – and *vairāgya* – desirelessness – are too heavy to bear for the modern *sādhaka-s* who want to be *sādhaka-s* without doing any *sādhanā.* People take pride in saying that they are practitioners of yoga though their practice may be at a very minimum level. It is our tendency to take pride in whatever little we do. That is the psychology of modern mind. We have interest but we are not intense. To do anything we have to be tempted. We need an incentive.

Therefore, I am adding a little more to these definitions. Let me put it as, *Yogaḥ duhkḥavṛtti nirodhaḥ II* – Yoga is restraint of the sorrows of *citta*

We all have pains, pinches, sorrows and hurts. At sometime or other we all have depression and dejection. We may hide inside and we may not like to express these externally, but all these are present in us and all of us want to get rid of our sorrows. Therefore, we need an incentive, a temptation to practise yoga in order to eradicate the sorrows.

Many people have a misunderstanding or misconception regarding the practice of yoga. They think that yoga is to be practised only when they suffer from disease. Whenever one claims that one is practising yoga, the question commonly asked is, "Why, what's wrong with you, are you not keeping well?" That is how yoga has become negatively popular. Many believe that yoga is practised only by those who are sick, or those who need to improve their health. I cannot blame people for this. It is through sickness, illness, physical and mental disease that a person develops sensitivity to sorrows and pains. These sorrows and pains force one to find a way to get rid of the problems and tempt one to take to yogic practices. Though the incentive might be trifling and negligible, it is not of minor importance.

There is a hidden cause behind disease, behind health problems, apart from the causes of disease claimed by medical science. Patañjali invites our attention to look at the root cause of disease.

The root cause of disease is within us. It is hidden in our own behaviour, our own habits, our character, our nature, our mental attitude, whether good or bad, right or wrong. Take for example, chocolate. We like chocolate and we eat and cherish it. But we do not know when it leaves an imprint on our teeth, our liver, making it sluggish or causing diabetes. Our own behaviour and character may add fuel to diabetes. It is only when we become aware of the danger of disease, that we embrace yoga.

Sage Patañjali knew these weaknesses and tendencies. He saw that man only searches the way when he has problems. Until problems and troubles arise, the will of man does not surface in the mind to find a way or a solution. Problems such as fear of disease, fear of suffering, fear of old age and the fear of death are there in every human being. Therefore, he says,

Heyaṁ duḥkham anāgatam – The sorrows which are yet to come can be avoided.

He assures us; promises us; that the pains which are yet to come, the problems which are in store for the future, the diseases which are waiting to arise, can be avoided and must be prevented. The sorrows and agonies can be kept away with the practice of yoga.

Lord Krishna too, smoothes the path of yoga with the following advice. He says,

Yuktāhāra vihārasya yuktaceṣṭasya karma-su I
yukta svapnāvabodhasya yogo bhavati duḥkhahā II

The conquest of sorrow is possible provided man regulates his diet, recreation of mind, performance of actions, sleep and wakefulness. Yoga helps one to get rid of the sorrows. If one regulates and balances life, the practice won't be so difficult. The path of yoga becomes smoother and easier to cross if one disciplines oneself. The path is not only open, but made smooth to practise for the sufferer.

Undoubtedly we are all keen to get rid of sorrow. Just analysing sorrow does not eradicate it. Through analysis you have to act so that you may find the root cause of sorrow hidden as *saṁskāra-s. Saṁskāra* is a very meaningful word; it means the accumulation of past actions and the culturing of oneself in the present life. Though we culture ourselves with good thoughts, good words and good behaviour, the *saṁskāra-s* of bad thoughts and wrong behaviour leave imprints behind in the form of impressions. The positive thoughts and behaviours leave positive impressions; negative or wrong thoughts leave negative impressions.

If the heart is to be cleansed and purified, a beginning has to be made by culturing the mind and culturing the consciousness. The process of culturing has two facets. One is to cultivate new *saṁskāra-s* which help to cleanse one's body, senses, mind, intellect, ego and consciousness. The other is to eradicate the old, unwanted and wrong *saṁskāra-s.*

However, the latent and hidden impressions which leave their imprints deep in the heart, deep in the core of the consciousness, cannot be easily washed off. These hidden impressions called *vāsanā-s* – desires – are unending, continuous and in-exhaustive. They are stored and imprinted in the memory from time immemorial. These imprints are what form our tendencies. The desires leave the imprints behind and the imprints ignite the desires again. This is how the cycle continues. If the imprints are the seeds, the desires are in the form of the tree. From every seed the tree grows and the tree gives seeds again. This is how the chain of tendencies continues.

Our inner tendencies cannot be easily changed. They haunt us not only in this life, but also in successive lives. Yoga is the only method that heals the wounds created by wrong or negative *saṁskāra-s* in the heart. It minimises the imprints of memories and desires and finally eradicates them. Yoga is the only way to cultivate new and positive imprints so that the onslaught of desire is lessened. Its practice cultivates new impressions which are corrective and conducive to take one towards the very core of the being. These are called yogic *saṁskāra-s.* The yogic *saṁskāra-s* free one from the sorrows and eradicate those *saṁskāra-s* which are antagonistic to the yogic *saṁskāra-s.* Finally a time comes, where all *saṁskāra-s* have to be restrained. This is what Patañjali says, when he speaks in the *Samādhi Pāda,* on *abhyāsa* and *vairāgya.*

One has to remove the opposing tendencies by cultivating suitable tendencies and finally, restrain all the tendencies. Yoga is a process of cleansing and eradicating the tendencies and imprints. This gives us one more definition, *Yogaḥ saṁskāravṛtti nirodhaḥ* – Yoga restrains the modifications of the *saṁskāra-s.*

The yogic path is such that the imprints are eradicated one by one with the new light of wisdom called *ṛtaṁbharā prajñā.* Finally, even this wisdom is relinquished. The weapon is first used to destroy and after the destruction the weapon too is relinquished. Similarly, the ultimate *saṁskāra,* that is *ṛtaṁbharā prajñā,* is used as a weapon to destroy the last residue of the impressions, finally the impression of *ṛtaṁbharā prajñā* is also left behind.

Ṛtambharā is a very beautiful, poetic word. The word indicates its profound weight and depth. It cannot be translated in a single word. *Ṛtaṁbharā* means a truth-bearing state. It is a matured state of the unalloyed wisdom of the intellect of the head and intelligence of the inner mind. *Prajñā* means intelligent awareness. *Ṛtaṁbharā prajñā* is the highest peak of intelligence. High on the icy peak of the Everest of wisdom, beyond this there remains nothing except the light of the soul. That is why I say,

Yogaḥ saṁskāravṛtti nirodhaḥ //

GOD AND MAN

All these definitions of yoga, whether the union between *jīvātman* and *paramātman,* the establishment of equanimity, the adoption of skillful action, the discipline and restraint of mental modifications, the eradication of sorrow and imprints of desires, make us aware of the fact that we want to be free from afflictions. We want to seek that which we lack. Here, man surely distinguishes himself from God. The difference between God and man makes man to realise the importance of yoga. Yoga links God and man, binding man to God. I want to remind you again that the word yoga is derived from the *Sanskṛt* root, *'yujir',* which means 'to bind' or 'to join' or 'to direct the attention'.

Whether one believes in God or not, the fact remains that man wants to be free from sorrows. He wants to find real and lasting happiness. He wants peace. He wants satisfaction. He wants to know about everything that he possibly can know about. Basically he is inquisitive; he is a seeker of knowledge. Even an illiterate person does not want to remain ignorant. There is a thirst for knowledge in him also. He wants to know and therefore, he seeks for knowledge. Compared to an educated person an illiterate person may seem to be uneducated, but there is still this tendency to seek knowledge. The instinct towards knowledge tempts a person to know more and more. Man knows that he is incomplete; therefore, his efforts are to know more. The more he knows, the more he realises how little he knows.

This inner human tendency to acquire knowledge forces the belief that there is a Complete Being, who knows everything; nothing is hidden from this Complete Being, who is free from sorrows. This Being is seen as no other than the Supreme. It is because of man's incomplete understanding and his search for knowledge that he accepts God.

Being imperfect, the more we try to march towards perfection the more we realise how far we are from perfection; how weak we are, how imperfect we are. Thus, we realise that we really are much less than God. God is the highest peak of knowledge for man. For him to know the Supreme is to know everything. His never ending effort is to search for the unknown, the ultimate, where knowledge terminates. When man reaches that peak, nothing remains to be known. The effort to become perfect ceases when the unknown is known.

The orthodox philosophical school of yoga accepts God. But what we need to understand is how Patañjali beautifully visualises and contrasts the picture of God and the picture of man.

We have already seen how a man is caught in the eternal desires – *vāsanā-s*. No one in this world is free from desires. The desires activate and motivate man to do *karma*. Man is action-oriented and cannot survive without *karma*. Not a single moment passes without action. Action whether physical or mental, is always there. Every action leaves its effect behind. Every action gives fruit, either good or bad. The fruit may be visible or non-visible. It could ripen immediately or later. The fruit of *karma* or action may be experienced after such a long gap that we are unable to trace or remember the action. The cause may be hidden in previous births, but the effects are experienced in the present and future lifetimes.

Lord Patañjali asks us to trace the root cause of every action. There is not a single action that occurs without some motivation. This motivation is hidden in affliction. The root cause of all actions and their fruits are hidden in the afflictions – the *kleśa-s.* So many unknown actions will be carried out for unknown reasons. But the basic cause will be hidden in the afflictions. The afflictions tempt one to act, react and interact.

With all his good qualities, man is still full of ignorance, pride, passion, enmity and tenacity. Though he has knowledge of the certainty of his death, he does not easily accept it. Due to his fear of death he clings to life, like a child clinging to its mother. He has no tolerance for pain. His pleasure seeking mind avoids pain. For him, pain is the greatest enemy. Avoiding pain leaves the imprint of hatred inside. Seeking pleasure leaves the mask of attachment within. Though attachment and aversion are opposite to each other, they have a firm root within us, leaving their imprints. This leads man into egocentricity, selfishness, pride and vanity. In the end he inevitably remains in the ocean of ignorance. Patañjali recognises it as the *pañca kleśa-s* – five afflictions. The *pañca kleśa-s* motivate man to do the *karma.* These five afflictions are ignorance or nescience, egoism, attachment, aversion and clinging to worldly life. If we try to analyse our actions we will find that each and every action is rooted in these afflictions.

We all know that energy cannot be destroyed. It is either transformed or transmitted. Similarly, though an action ends, their imprints do not. Every action leaves its mark or imprint in the person who carries out the act. This is how man accumulates imprints. The *saṁskāra-s* of *karma* – imprints of actions – are not only from the present life but also from past lives, rooted in afflictions. The reservoir of *karma* is ever full, since the unfathomable afflictions are the base for this reservoir. Birth, the span and experience of life which we call fate or destiny, are the sprouts of these past *karma-s.* The effort to experience the world is already destined. We are forced to experience the world of pleasure and pain since the seeds are already there. This is the limitation of human beings.

God, however, is free from afflictions, conflicts and unaffected by actions. He is also free from the fruits of actions and thus untouched by cause and effect. Yet, He has unquestionable and unparalleled potentiality. He is omnipotent. Being free from afflictions He has no bondage to birth and death. He is omnipresent. He is eternal.

He is the seed or origin of all knowledge. His knowledge cannot be surpassed or excelled. He is the first and foremost *Guru,* the *Guru* of *Guru-s,* without any condition to place or time. He is omniscient. He is the ocean of knowledge.

Patañjali names this special *puruṣa* as *'Puruṣa Viśeṣa'* or God a Unique Universal Soul.

Well! God for this reason alone, is recognised by the *praṇava* – *auṁ*. *Auṁ* is considered to be the symbol of Divinity. *Praṇava* stands for praise of divine fulfilment. *Auṁ* is composed of three syllables *a*, *u* and *ṁ*. No language is complete without the sound of these three syllables. *Auṁ* is the seed from which all words and languages spring. *Auṁ* is considered to be *śabda-Brahman* – the word of God, a Universal Sound.

It is interesting to see that Patañjali's *Īśvara* is not a personified or anthropomorphic God. In *Sanskṛt*, *Īśvara* means God. The word indicates supremacy. The word *aiśvarya* is hidden in *Īśvara*. *Aiśvarya* means glory. The one who has unexcelled, insurmountable and unparalleled glory is called *Īśvara*. The whole universe belongs to Him. He owns the universe. When Patañjali calls God with the words *Puruṣa Viśeṣa*, he is pointing out that God is a distinct *puruṣa* compared to human beings.

Puruṣa means a human being. It also means soul. *Puri śete iti puruṣa Ilḥ.* The word *puri* means town or city. It indicates the body. *Śete* means to dwell. *Puruṣa* is the one who dwells in the city of the body and hence this dweller is the soul. The soul exists in all the living beings, but *puruṣa viśeṣa* is specified as distinct from the rest of the souls since God is a distinct *puruṣa* – *Puruṣa Viśeṣa*.

Why did *Patañjali* think of *Īśvara?* Why did he bring in this topic at all? He could have proceeded without referring to *Īśvara*. Did he refer to *Īśvara* because of our limitations, the limitations of human beings?

There are two main points by which one can recognise *Īśvara* – God. First of all, man is incomplete, imperfect and has limitations. Whereas *Īśvara* is complete, perfect and boundlessly glorious. Secondly, though man has limitations, Patañjali does not want him to lose faith in himself and his own efforts. He wants him to direct all his efforts and energy to aim at God. Let us look into this point clearly.

Patañjali introduces *Īśvara* to us at the right place. He invites our attention on our own efforts. He does not say to depend totally on God. Rather, he asks us to trust our own efforts, to change ourselves by our own efforts and to apply our efforts with a positive attitude. He does not make us helpless, negative, or totally dependent on God by disregarding and disrespecting our own potency.

Patañjali says, "Have full faith in yourself. Trust yourself and your efforts. Be confident. Apply your efforts totally, with full physical, moral, mental, intellectual and spiritual strength. Have a good store of memory". Memory depends upon your involvement in practice; your keenness to achieve the goal; your power to absorb; your efforts, alertness and awareness.

At this point, you are not only eager but also intense. Here, *Patañjali* introduces you to the concept of *Īśvara* – God as *Puruṣa Viśeṣa*. He asks you to surrender yourself to God. He asks you to meditate on God, to deposit all your efforts and achievements in that omnipotent *Īśvara*. Let there be complete access to *Īśvara*, because *Īśvara* is a *yoga-kāraka*, an establisher of yoga. He is *Yogeśvara*, the Lord of Yoga. He is *sarvajñabīja*, the seed of all knowledge. Nothing will be known without His blessings. The knowledge that we earn and gain is imbibed from the *sarvajña*, the God who knows everything, the God who is the Universe of Knowledge.

The main human weakness is the ego. The ego is the biggest hurdle on the path of knowledge. Man is proud of all his achievements. Certainly, he can be proud of all that he has gained and achieved through his efforts. But with all his achievements, the moment he realises that he could be wrong, that his actions could be faulty and his knowledge limited, he begins to accept God. He drops his ego at the exact point where he realises his limits. He realises that he is less than God. And *Patañjali* introduces God to him at this threshold.

Patañjali asks the pupils and followers of yoga to do *Īśvara praṇidhāna*. *Praṇidhāna* means total concentration. It is the state of *ekāgratā*. *Eka*, means one and alone. It is a unique state. *Agra* means the first or the base that is the soul. Conscious attention on this one point – the soul – is *ekāgratā*. Consciousness undergoes transformation with the practice of yoga. Patañjali wants the *sādhaka* to move the consciousness from this one-pointed attention of the soul towards God-pointed attention. This is *Īśvara praṇidhāna*. This *praṇidhāna* state of consciousness is a very refined, permanent, everlasting state. To achieve this state, *Patañjali* asks us to discipline ourselves by surrender, prayers and worship of God in the moral practice of *niyama*. He wants us to surrender the fruits of our actions when we adopt yoga with its discipline and practices. Though we become adepts in yoga, still the ego accompanies us as a companion; therefore, he asks us to concentrate only on God. Patañjali asks us to drop the ego and let go of all objects, thoughts and desires that squeezes and sucks our energy and consciousness – *citta* – like a leech that sucks the blood. This is how the sense of *Īśvara praṇidhāna* changes at different levels of *sādhanā*.

We are caught up in the cycles of *sukha* and *duḥkha* – joy and sorrow, pleasure and pain, *māna* and *apamāna* – honour and dishonour, *jaya* and *parājaya* – success and failure, *ādara* and *anādara* – respect and disrespect, *ūṣṇa* and *śīta* – heat and cold, *janma, jarā* and *mṛtyū* – birth, old age and death. *Īśvara* is not caught in these dualities. *Īśvara* is unaffected, beyond all afflictions, beyond all actions and beyond the fruits of actions. *Īśvara* is never exhausted and is ever existing.

POLLUTION IN ACTION

Let us know our own weaknesses. Our actions and thoughts are mixed with our feelings, limited understanding and our lack of knowledge. We are not sure about what we do. We are doubtful about our own actions and fruits. We are indecisive. Often we are provoked to act out of greed, anger, delusion, malice and desire. Aren't we?

We have the desire to achieve something. We compete with each other. We compare ourselves with others. We do, because others do. We want to possess of what others have. We are jealous of what others have and we want to have that. Whether the actions are constructive or destructive, there is always a tinge of selfishness. Our mind acts and reacts with selfish motives. This is ambitiousness. What could be the imprint on us of all these actions tainted with such blemishes? Since the actions are tainted, the imprints are also tainted. Every action with its mental attitude leaves behind imprints of a similar quality and we are caught in them.

It has been said that the most highly developed brain is the brain of human beings. We like to consider ourselves to be the most intellectually developed animal. But, can we trust our intelligence? Sometimes, we are in fact so dull that we go blank. Sometimes we are so lazy that we don't want to exert our brain, our intelligence. Sometimes our ambitious mind gets agitated and at other times it lacks any inner drive or urge. At such junctures the mind oscillates. Surprisingly at times we experience single-pointed attention. We experience restraint and control. In other words, I would say that our intelligence has its own moods and modes.

Our intelligence shows five characteristics or properties. It acts according to the projection of these properties, showing dullness, negligence, agitation, one-pointedness or restraint. That is *mūḍha, kṣipta, vikṣipta, ekāgra* and *niruddha,* respectively. Consciousness is categorised according to these five characteristic intellectual behaviours.

This explains how every action of ours' is influenced by complicated moods and modes of intelligence. Action is polluted by mental attitudes and feelings such as anger, desire, greed, delusion, infatuation, jealousy and pride. If our nature is violent, dishonest, possessive, unchaste or greedy, it influences the action that is done, induced to do or permitted to do. Patañjali refers to these as *kṛta, kārita* and *anumodita.* All these actions, whether *kṛta-karma, kārita-karma* or *anumodita-karma* depend upon the characteristic of intelligence and our past imprints.

All these may seem to be complicated, but they do exist. The *karma-s* may seem to be pure and perfect from outside, but they are polluted and in turn, pollute us. Nevertheless, we cannot avoid the *karma-s,* even though they are polluted, simply because a man is a *karma puruṣa* – born of his own *karma.* He is built up of his own *karma.* He has to do *karma.* He cannot abandon *karma.* He cannot discard his duties. He cannot avoid this inborn nature of doing duty. Lord Krishna calls this inborn nature of doing one's duty as *svadharma*. *Sva* means one's own and *dharma* means duty. *Dharma* means a religious duty. Now, what is this religious duty? Is it a duty of a man-made religion? No! Certainly not. *Dharma* is a righteous and virtuous duty. However, with all these weaknesses; we have to purify ourselves by doing our duty that is right and honourable. We have to think and change our mental attitude so that we do our duty with competence. As we begin to cleanse ourselves our attitudes, our work, our actions and intentions behind our actions begin to get purified.

We are always proud to say that we are independent but we are all caught in our *karma*. For instance we alone are responsible for *kṛta-karma* or direct action; whereas *kārita-karma,* we are induced and forced through others to do, while in *anumodita-karma,* we may not participate but give consent to do the work.

The *kṛta-karma* is certainly done by us. It is attempted by us. We are the doers. We are wholly and solely responsible for our *kṛta-karma-s*. Yet the *kṛta-karma-s* done by us may not be pure. These actions of ours are polluted and therefore distorted, because these actions are often done with a selfish motive or with the desire to gain name, fame and fortune. Often these actions are done out of lust, anger or sometimes out of revenge. There is always a reason behind each *kṛta-karma*. We can give a reason for each *karma* from an intellectual point of view but rarely do we undertake our duties with a pure intention.

Though we may begin to work with a pure intention but at a certain point unknowingly, the intention gets polluted and mixed up with our selfish emotions. That is how *kṛta-karma* leaves its track of dust behind and the duty becomes dirty.

With the *kārita-karma* or induced action, one does not realise that one has been caught, as someone else ordered or induced one to do the duty. We are made to get tempted to do the work. We are enticed by someone's words or influences. We act as they direct us and we are caught and get entangled. We may feel that we are not responsible for such acts and that we are just the catalysts. But it is not true. Since we are the doers and the work has been influenced to be done by someone else, we are tempted to do that which has the tinge of blemish. This imprint of blemish is left behind and we have to pay for it.

In *anumodita-karma,* somebody gives consent and we carry out the duty. We do not question our own action. We are satisfied that someone has given consent, we forget to think either directly or indirectly, whether the person who gave the consent had a tinged or clear intelligence. If that person's intelligence is tainted, our actions get tainted. On the other hand we may give the consent,

Manusyāṇām sahasreṣu kaścidyatati siddhaye I
yatatāmapi siddhīnām kaścinmām vetti tattvataḥ II

Lord Krishna says, "One among thousands of men strives to realise Me; and of those striving *yogi-s,* some rare ones who devote themselves exclusively to Me, know Me in reality." We are all God-seekers; very few are God-seers.

Let us be one of those thousands. Let us strive and put in our efforts. We have to purify ourselves with righteous and virtuous duty. We have to be one of those rare ones who really want to know the eternal *Puruṣa*. If we have to reach the state of a *siddha puruṣa* then we have to practise with intense enthusiasm passionately like a blazing fire known as *tapas*. We have to practise yoga not only uninterruptedly but with attentive reflection and profound meditation as *abhyāsa*. At the same time we have to learn to develop *vairāgya* – non-attachment and renounce that which obstructs practice. In other words, we have to train our body, mind and intellect to understand the various facets of *prakṛti*. We have to know how to chisel the principles of *prakṛti* in order to shape our natural tendencies of *prakṛti*.

PURUṢA AND *PRAKṚTI*

We saw the difference between *puruṣa* and *Puruṣa Viśeṣa*, man and God. The human being and the Supreme Being. Now we have to see the difference between *puruṣa* and *prakṛti*, the soul and matter, the subject and the object, the being and the becoming.

Yoga is the path and *prakṛti* is the vehicle. It is in the vehicle of *prakṛti*, that we have to tread the path of yoga in order to understand *puruṣa* – the soul. *Prakṛti* is the greatest God-given

Table 1: Cosmogony - Chart on Creation

- *Sriṣṭi Karta & Sriṣṭikrama*
  - God, Creator, *Parama Puruṣa, Puruṣa Viśeṣa, Sriṣṭi Karta, Viśvacaitana Puruṣa, Antaryāmi,* Supreme Soul
    - *Sriṣṭikrama* or Order Of Creation
      - *Puruṣa*
        - Immortal Soul (BIG SELF)
          Jjivātma - *Antaḥkaraṇa*
          (Mortal self or small self) *Dharmendriya* (sense of conscience)
      - *Viśvacaitanya Śakti*
        - *Panca Prāṇa* corresponding to *bhuta-s*
          - *Vyāna*
          - *Udāna*
          - *Samāna*
          - *Prāṇa*
          - *Apāna*
      - *Mulaprakṛti* with *Guṇa-s* or Qualities
        - *Sattva* (Illumination)
        - *Rajas* (Motion+ Action)
        - *Tamas* (Dormancy /Inertia)
        - *Mahat* (Cosmic consciousness or intelligence)
          - *Citta* (Individual Consciousness)
            - *Manas* (Mind)
            - *Buddhi* (Intelligence)
            - *Ahaṁkāra* (I-maker)
            - *Jñānendriya-s* (senses of perception) feedback systems
              - Ears
              - Skin
              - Eyes
              - Tongue
              - Nose
            - *Karmendriya-s* (organs of action)
              - Arms
              - Legs
              - Mouth
              - Generatory organ
              - Excretory organ
        - *Panca Tanmātra*
          - *Śabdha*
          - *Sparṣa*
          - *Rupa*
          - *Rasa*
          - *Gandha*
        - *Panca Bhuta*
          - *Ākāśa* (Ether)
          - *Vāyu* (Air)
          - *Tej* (Fire)
          - *Āp* (Water)
          - *Pṛthvi* (Earth)

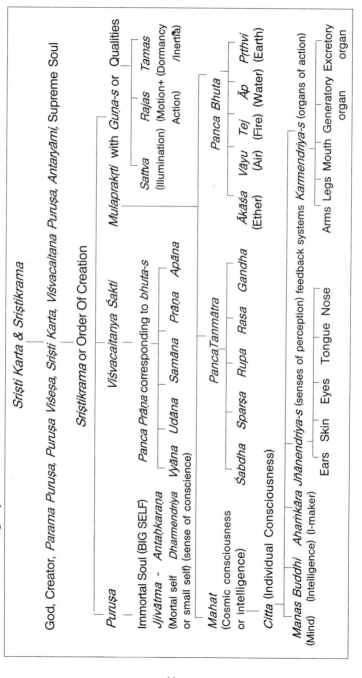

gift to all of us. Yoga teaches us to utilise *prakṛti* so that through *prakṛti* we transform ourselves to reach its Lord – the *Puruṣa.* Therefore, let us know about *prakṛti.*

The relationship between *puruṣa* and *prakṛti* is very complex and puzzling. *Patañjali* unfolds this relationship in a very delicate way. Perhaps he has chosen a right place and a right time to explain *prakṛti* and *puruṣa.* The *Sādhana Pāda* of the *Yoga Sūtra-s* is devoted to this topic for the simple reason that unless one knows *prakṛti* and *puruṣa* and their inter-relationship, *sādhanā* does not make any sense. Therefore, practitioners of yoga are compelled to know about *puruṣa* and *prakṛti.*

Table 2. - The Three Separate Entities

	God	Man	Nature
1	*Īśvara* *Puruṣa Viśeṣa*	*Puruṣa*	*Prakṛti*
2	*Paramātmā*	*Jīvātmā*	———
3	Universal Soul	Individual self	Universe Inanimate World
4	Supreme	———	———
5	God	*Draṣṭā*	*Dṛśya*
6	———	Seer	Seen

Prakṛti means nature. Nature is vast. It includes the whole universe – the known, the unknown, the Earth and the Solar systems.

Everything from the smallest insect to the number of solar systems that are unknown to us are included in *prakṛti*.

Puruṣa and *prakṛti* are both eternal, infinite entities. *Puruṣa* or the soul, is imperishable. The weapons cannot cut nor fire can burn it, water cannot wet it nor can wind dry it. But *prakṛti* or nature though eternal is changeable and perishable. *Prakṛti* evolves. Evolution is its characteristic. On the other hand *puruṣa* – the soul – is unchangeable.

DRAṢṬĀ AND DṚŚYA

What is in macrocosm or *brahmāṇḍa* is in microcosm or *piṇḍāṇḍa*. As such, we, as human beings are part and parcel of *prakṛti* or nature, and therefore it is not only necessary but our duty to know it. This universe is so vast, that it is not possible for us to grasp it through our perception. Whatever we see, know or witness is limited. Therefore, *Patañjali* uses the word *draṣṭā* for *puruṣa*, which means the seer; and *dṛśya* for *prakṛti*, which means the seen. Though the word *draṣṭā* stands for *puruṣa* and *dṛśya* for *prakṛti*, the words are thoughtfully used by Patañjali. As the seer acts as the seeker in us, we have limitations; because the seer becomes the seeker on account of our ignorance, the seer as seeker sees as the intelligence projects. This seer is the individual self or *jīvātmā* and the seen is the consciousness – *citta*, a miniature of cosmic intelligence *(mahat)* within us, as individual intelligence.

Patañjali does not say that one has to study the whole of *prakṛti.* Rather, one has to study and understand the view that comes in the sphere of vision for a viewer. When we go to the peak of a mountain, we have a better view than from the ground level. An aerial view is much broader and wider than the view at ground level. Similarly, as the seer begins to see the seen clearly, or as the *draṣṭā* begins to see *dṛśya* very clearly, the vision becomes wider for the seer. When the consciousness is unclean, polluted and contaminated by the mixture of thoughts and experiences, its vision, even at the eye level, will not be clear. But if the consciousness is clear and unpolluted, then it is just like seeing clearly from the peak of a mountain.

With this idea in mind, *Patañjali* uses the 'seer' and the 'seen' as appropriate words for *'puruṣa'* and *'prakṛti'* or the consciousness in us. He uses *'draṣṭā'* for the seer and *'dṛśya'* for the seen. *Draṣṭā* means the seer and *dṛśya* means the potential power to see. The seer is a viewer and the seen is a view. Vision is limited to the physical eyes. The eyes see only up to the level that they can see. But if we wish to see more, certainly we can exert our intelligence to see a little further and that is how we make use of the instrument of the *dṛśya,* the power of viewing. Since *puruṣa* or *draṣṭā* is a seer he has the power to see. This power is called the *dṛk-śakti* of *puruṣa.* On the other hand *prakṛti* is called *darśana-śakti.* It cannot see but it can show.

I will use the analogy of the television set. It has a full capacity to project. It shows but it cannot see itself as it is an instrument in someone's hands. Similarly, we have within us a system like the television set and that is our consciousness. Consciousness is *citta*. This instrument called *citta* gathers all the views, all the experiences and knowledge. Just as the television set has different channels, the *citta* too has different channels. The eyes that see are one channel, the ears that hear are another, so too, the tongue that tastes, the skin that feels the touch and the nose that smells, are the other channels. Further, the intellect which thinks, the mind which gathers experiences, the memory that can remember are all channels. Though this system of consciousness gathers all types of knowledge, being insentient it shows or projects this gathered knowledge to the soul – the seer – and the seer sees. This power of showing, power of projecting is *darśana-śakti* and the power of seeing whatever has been projected, is *dṛk-śakti*. In other words, the *dṛśya* has the power of viewing like a television set, therefore, it is seen. The seer sees the seen. The potential power of the seer and the seen is recognised as *dṛk-śakti* and *darśana-śakti*. *Śakti* is a potential power. These two powers are functional powers.

Suppose, I have not switched on the television set, then I will not see anything and I realise that the television set is not on. Similarly, the seer sees only if the seen is showing. Even if the television set is not on, it has the potential to show and as soon as it is switched on or charged with the electric current, it begins to show. As far as the television set is concerned, its charging is through the energy of electricity. In our own system, *draṣṭā* has this power to charge at once. The moment the seer begins to see the television set of consciousness, the seen, is on and when the seer does not see the television set, the consciousness is off. As the screen of the television set gets the light, it means the television is on. Similarly, when the light is thrown on the screen of consciousness by the seer to see, the seer sees the consciousness. This television set within is so sensitive that it always appears to be in a tuned state. The inner television set is charged in the minutest fraction of a second hence, the consciousness begins to project all that it has gathered at once. This *darśana-śakti* of *citta* is highly sensitive. It is so quick to project the view, its speed, its sensitivity and its state of immediate projection, makes it proud of itself. This pride is called *asmitā*. Can a television set be proud of itself, proud of its potency? Can a telephone be proud of itself and say that it is a great messenger? No! Certainly not! These devices cannot take pride in their functions. Because these devices cannot do anything on their own, they have to be handled by somebody, utilised by someone.

However, consciousness – *citta,* which is an instrument of the *'citi'* – another word for the seer, takes pride in its functional job. It thinks that it is the seer which in fact is nothing but a television set that thinks as though it has its own power to view and power to show. This pride is *asmitā* or the I-maker.

The seer has *dṛk-śakti* and the seen has *darśana-śakti*. The instrumental or functional power identifies itself with the power of the seen. The *darśana-śakti* thinks that it is *dṛk-śakti*. This is a kind of deliberate mistake, a deliberate misidentification on the part of the seen projecting itself as though it is the seer. When the seen feels that it is the seer it becomes *asmitā*. Actually *asmitā* is an imposter of the seer. Here, I will explain its literal meaning to you, which makes you to understand *asmitā* in much clearer terms. *Asmi* means to be. The seen projects itself as though it is a seer. This kind of it's 'to-be-ness' is called *asmitā*.

CONJUNCTION AND DISSOCIATION

The seer and the seen are very close to each other as though they are identical twins. But this is an inadequate example. Twins exist separately and lead their lives separately. As far as the seer and the seen are concerned, they are associated very closely to each other. As they seem to be one, yoga is meant to dissociate this conjunction.

However, this conjunction between *draṣṭā* and *dṛśya* not only seems to be permanent but also painful. *Patañjali* says the conjunction between the seer and the seen is the cause of suffering.

Draṣṭṛdṛśyayoḥ saṁyogaḥ heyahetuḥ II

However, this conjunction is not permanent. If the conjunction was permanent then the pains too would be permanent. But *Patañjali* says there is a solution and that the pains can and are to be eradicated.

Heyaṁ duḥkham anāgatam II

Patañjali promises us that the pains which are yet to come, which are waiting to cause suffering can be avoided. We do not know what is in store for us in the future, but we can still obstruct and put a brake or minimise the future pains. This is a very concrete, positive approach of *Patañjali*. He says, "Work through yoga and build up a defensive power.

Well, it is a fact that the conjunction between *prakṛti* and *puruṣa* is the cause of suffering. There is a saying: "Whatever happens, happens for the good". The pains and sufferings may be the signs to show us a path that leads us towards the good.

This conjunction that is causing pain may prove to be friendly or may turn out to be our enemy. Let us try to understand the nature of this peculiar conjunction. I have already said that a misidentification between the power of the seer and the power of the seen appearing as one, causes pride to sprout from within. *Patañjali* says that this conjunction between the seer and the seen causes pain. However, he says that the pain can be eradicated. There is a remedy for this contagious union and this remedy is hidden in the cause itself. If the cause is analysed and realised, then the remedy as answer can be found out.

Svasvāmiśaktyoḥ svarūpopaladhihetuḥ saṁyogaḥ II

Prakṛti is there to help the *puruṣa* to discover his own nature. This conjunction is meant for the seer to discover his own true nature. The seer has the power of owning, known as *svāmi-śakti* and the seen has the power to be owned called *sva-śakti. Svāmi* means the owner and *sva* means to be owned. It is also possible that the contact of the seer with the seen might become not only meaningful, but also purposeful. The purpose of this contact once unfolded, changes the whole picture on life as well as in the art of living. The doubts and misunderstandings and misconceptions disappear and in their places friendship, loveliness and liveliness set in. The seer recognises his own power and realises that he

Table 3. - The Power of the Seer and the Seen

THE HUMAN BEING				
Seer	**+**	**Seen**	**=**	**Conjunction**
dṛaṣṭā	+	*dṛśya*	=	experience and emancipation *(bhoga & apavarga)*
dṛk-śakti	+	*darśana-śakti*	=	'I' consciousness *(asmitā)*
svāmi-śakti	+	*sva-śakti*	=	discovery of seer's true nature *(svarūpopalabdhi)*

owns the seen. The seen becomes automatically submissive. As the seer owns the seen, where then is the place for pride or *asmitā?*

If the seer evolves, then he uses the instruments of the seen judiciously. But if the seer is not evolved, then he identifies himself with the seen. The seer gets involved in the seen. This involvement is explained by *Patañjali* as, *Vṛtti sārūpyam itaratra II*

At other times the seer gets caught by the seen and identifies with the fluctuating thoughts of the consciousness. The seer identifies himself with the thought-waves or *citta-vṛtti-s* and gets caught in mental modifications. A clean and pure seer enticed by the seen gets entangled in these thought-waves of the seen. This involvement of the seer makes the seer to cherish sensual pleasures, or *bhoga,* while its non-involvement leads one towards auspicious moments of goodness or yoga. Its involvement is temporal experience and its non-involvement is the experience of the auspicious state of emancipation and beatitude.

When the seer is free from these shackles, these entanglements are no more enticed by the seen,then the seer becomes a *kṛtārthan. Kṛtārthan* means the one who is successful, whose purpose has been fulfilled, who has fulfilled his duties and obtained the ultimate aim of life – *mokṣa* or freedom and beatitude.

The seer becomes a *kṛtārthan* because the seen ceases to exist for him. The *prakṛti* is eternal. It never vanishes. But for the *kṛtārthan,* it fades away for him. This right conjunction transforms the seen to be a seer. From now on the seer is no more a seeker but a seer.

BONDAGE OR FREEDOM?

It is essential for the practitioner of yoga to remember that nature plays a dual role. It can cause either bondage or freedom. Nature being an instrument, it depends upon how the user makes use of it. Yoga clearly mentions that nature exists in order to serve the soul. The nature or the seen exists to serve the seer or the *puruṣa.*

Just like the television set, which is ever ready to serve its master whenever he switches it on, so is nature. The television not only entertains the viewer but also helps him in enhancing his knowledge of the world and its situations. It depends on the viewer to choose to open the channel of the emancipating knowledge or the channel of entertainment. Similarly, the nature can channel the knowledge to free the seer from bondage or it may bind the seer with worldly enjoyments and entertainments. If the seer or the viewer is a *kṛtārthan,* when he attains the end-aim in life, he need not open any channel of nature's enticing attractions since his hunger for entertainment has faded and the thirst for knowledge is quenched. The seen disappears the moment its job is over. If the seer is caught in the web of worldly attractions, then it binds the seer completely and then it becomes impossible for the seer to escape from the seen.

The body needs the seer and the seer needs the body for expressions and experiences. Hence, the seer cannot escape from the seen and the seen cannot escape from the seer. The yogic method is certainly not a method of escapism. It is a device that removes thorns on the path of freedom from natrure. It gives strength to cross the hurdles of nature's enticements and generates energy for overcoming the physical, moral, mental, intellectual and spiritual obstacles, so that the disparity between the seer and the seen is removed. Yoga acts as the instrument for both to become pure.

Newly married couples do not think of anyone else or anything else except each other. For the bride, the bridegroom is everything and for the bridegroom, the bride is everything. For them, the rest of the world is absent. In a similar manner when the thorns, the hurdles, the obstacles and the impediments, which stand between the seer and the seen are removed, the seer exists for the seen alone and the seen exists for the seer alone. The seen is like a pure mirror. The seer looks into that mirror of the seen and sees his own true reflection.

We all know that in case the mirror is not clean, it does not clearly reflect the image. The mirror of the seen is covered with vapour and dust. We need to clean the mirror. Or if the mirror runs out of mercury, it cannot reflect the image clearly. The mirror needs 'mirroring'.

Like the mirror that is covered with dust cannot reflect well, we have to know that the consciousness accumulates dust and vapour of nature's qualities. We need to polish the consciousness to be free from the qualities or *guṇa-s* of nature namely *sattva*

Table 4. - The Reflection

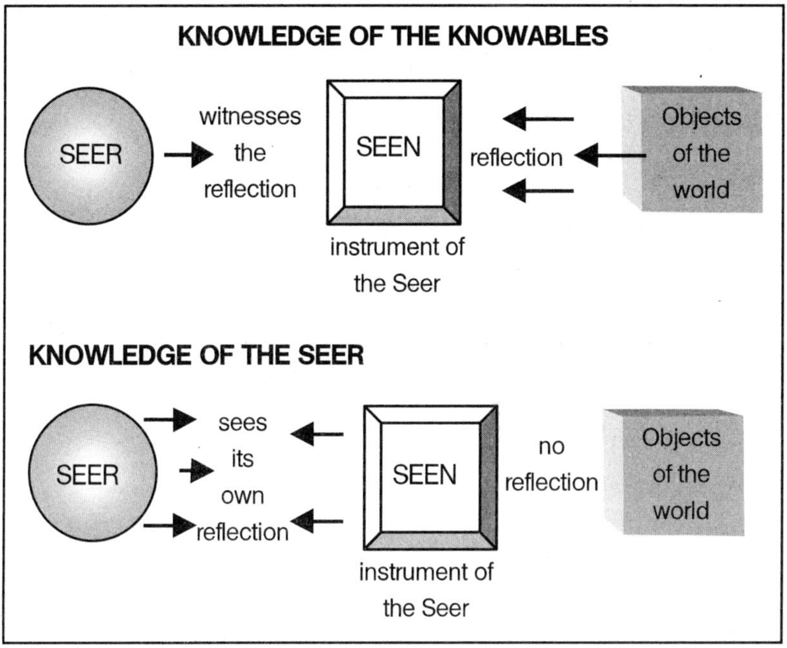

(illumination), *rajas* (vibrancy) and *tamas* (inertia), so that it reflects the seer and nothing else. Let us see how to clean the mirror of consciousness which reflects and re-reflects on body and soul. What kind of dust gathers and covers it?

We need to know how to clean this mirror and what method to use. To clean a mirror, sometimes we need a dry cloth and sometimes a wet cloth. Sometimes we have to sprinkle water to clean it or use soap or solvents. Similarly, in the yogic method, we have to use various methods to remove dust that gathers and covers the consciousness. In order to clean the mirror, it may need only water and polishing, or it may require detergents or it may require wet cleaning or dry cleaning. In the same way, various methods and techniques are involved in yoga to clear the dust of the consciousness. We have to see which kind of dust is there and decide which method we have to use to clean it.

Therefore, let us first sort out the dust in order to know its type. This unclean dust or rubbish is recognised by Patañjali as *vṛtti-s* – the mental modifications, *kleśa-s* – the afflictions and *antarāya-s* – the obstacles or impediments. The method of cleaning is *abhyāsa* and *vairāgya.* Let us first see the pollution, the dust and blemishes that are gathered which saturate the consciousness.

Now we have known and understood the difference between God and man as well as man and nature. Though all these three are separate entities, yet these three are not only meant for each other, but dependent on each other. Man is in the centre. He has two objects in front of him, namely, *prakṛti* – the field, and the seer – the fielder. It depends entirely on his will and wish to decide which one he wants to choose, whether to choose God – *Puruṣa Viśeśa* – the eternal and unmoveable as the highest aim; or nature – *prakṛti* – the eternal world which is everchanging. If he chooses to aim at *Puruṣa Viśeṣa,* then he is led towards emancipation and if he chooses to aim at *prakṛti,* then he ends up in bondage.

For example, Patañjali says,

draṣṭṛdṛśyayoḥ saṁyogaḥ heyahetuḥ II (*Y.S.,* II.17)

It means that the cause of pain is on account of the association or identification of the seer with the seen and says that the remedy is in its disassociation. This *sūtra* indirectly conveys that nature can be a friend or a foe of the seer as its association causes pains and sorrows.

These two aims seem to be absolutely separate and opposite to each other. But yogic discipline associates these two to make man a man and not to mar or spoil man. Man cannot afford to be choosy, according to his own whims and fancies. The selections or choices that man makes is always relative since it depends on his own likes and dislikes, wants and non-wants, need and greed. In a way, he is like a chameleon. As a chameleon changes its colour, man too can be churlish and selfish changing his tastes, his thoughts, his faith, his beliefs, his aims and his course of action. However, he has to make his decision soon, not according to his tastes, likes and dislikes, but with discriminative discernment, willpower and self-discipline to march towards emancipation or freedom from bondage.

Human birth is the rarest of all the rare gifts. It is the blessing of God and good *karma* that sanctions a human birth. The freedom of *karma* is given to us with a discriminative power for discretion. We have to make good use of this discriminative intellectual power as a great chance to plan our destiny and we have to build that destiny with good *karma-s.* This chance is not given to animals, birds or trees but only to man.

As human beings we are intelligent creatures. This intelligence is a wealth which we own, provided we use this wealth judiciously. The wealth is lost if we use it injudiciously. If we use the intelligence judiciously it can guide and lead us for our own betterment and evolution. *Citta* can be a friend when used judiciously and it becomes a foe if used injudiciously.

Therefore, in the beginning, the *citta* is caught in a tug of war between temporal enjoyments *(bhoga)* and eternal unalloyed and unbiased bliss. Nature pulls the consciousness towards the pleasures of the world on one side or towards the Self or the *jīvātman,* on the other. On one side man's consciousness is pulled towards bondage and on the other towards emancipation. Therefore, a mere decision is not of any use. Discriminative discernment is required to convert the foe, which mars the progress of man, to be its friend in order to cross over the bank of bondage through the bridge of discriminative intelligence towards eternal freedom. We know that the friend in need is a friend in deed. *Prakṛti* is a friend, not merely when one is in need, but a friend who is ready to die for us. *Prakṛti* is ready to sacrifice its own existence for *puruṣa.* Therefore, it is worth our while to change the qualities of nature which act as a foe, into a friend and this change is possible. It is possible with practice – *abhyāsa.* With *abhyāsa* we convert the *citta* to become a bosom friend serving us until the end, until we reach the final goal. The moment we reach the goal this bosom friend of ours departs with gratitude. It disappears since it has done its job; done its service.

It says, "I am no more for you, my dear soul, goodbye". But as long as the goal is not reached, it says "My dear friend, I am here for your sake alone". The servile nature of *prakṛti* is ever ready to serve other *puruṣa-s* again according to the will and wish of the *puruṣa-s,* either for bondage or emancipation. That is why it is not destroyed for average people.

Kṛtārthaṁ prati naṣṭam api anaṣṭaṁ tadanya sādhāraṇatvāt // (*Y.S.,* II.22)

It means, "The relationship with nature ceases for emancipated beings, as its purpose has been fulfilled, but its processes continues to affect others". *Prakṛti* is an eternal entity, who serves us in both ways. If we want to enjoy life, *prakṛti* helps us. We enjoy the worldly pleasures through this instrument. If we want emancipation, then it is the same *prakṛti* which helps us.

See how the compassionate Patañjali lifts the aspirant from the negative thoughts which he dealt in *Y.S.,* II.17 towards positive approach by saying that

sva svāmi śaktyoḥ svarūpopalabdhi hetuḥ saṁyogaḥ // (*Y.S.,* II.23)

It means the association or conjunction between the seer and the seen is for the seer to find out his own true nature.

We have now discussed how the seer and the seen are conjunct and we saw that the seen helps the seer to dissociate himself from the seen. Their conjunction is not aimless. The seen has the nature to be in conjunction with the seer. If this conjunction is used advertently, then it is *abhyāsa* and as such, the advertent conjunction leads one towards dissociation. When the seer and the seen are dis-juncted or dissociated, then it is *vairāgya.* But, before we proceed to know *abhyāsa* and *vairāgya,* let us see the result of inadvertent utilisation of this conjunction. Man has two goals by his side yoga or liberation – *bhoga* or bondage. Yoga is to unite man with God and *bhoga* is to unite him with worldly experiences. The *vaidika* terminology for these two goals is expressed as *śreyas* and *preyas. Śreyas* is pure bliss, happiness of the soul and *preyas* is worldly enjoyment. The synonym for these two approaches of the human mind is recognised as the path of *niśreyas or beyond virtues and moral merits* and *abhyudaya or elevation, prosperity and happiness.*

The *bhoga, preyas* or *abhyudaya,* shows that our human nature is attached more towards worldly enjoyments. Invariably it is down-to-earth nature in all of us. Let us not pretend about this. Unless we accept our hidden nature we cannot understand the other side of us which is *śreyas* or *niśreyas.* In order to understand this auspicious living, we need the practical aspect of the practical approach towards yoga. As we are caught up in worldly enjoyments, we need to transform ourselves to free ourselves from these non-permanent enjoyments and yoga is the only gateway that guides us practically freeing us from the clutches of worldly enjoyments.

Having known the origin of worldly life through the conjunction of the seer with the seen, we often misuse it due to our ignorance or arrogance and our problems begin from here. This misuse of the conjunction of the seen with the seer generates *vṛtti-s, kleśa-s* and *antarāya-s.*

Table 5. - The Accumulation of Dust and Dirt on the *Citta*

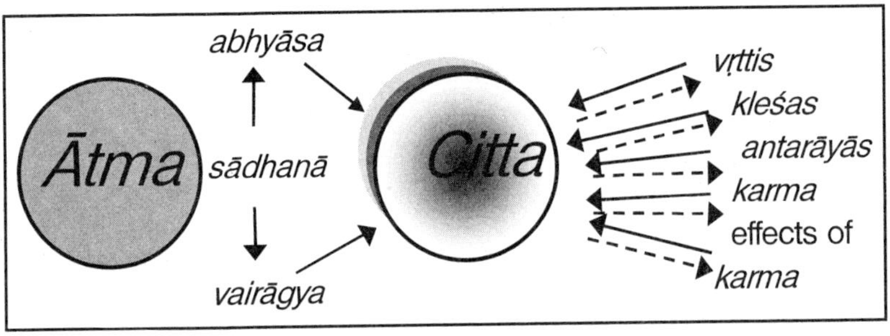

As a thorn is removed by using another thorn-like instrument, we need to use the *vṛtti-s* themselves to remove the *vṛtti-s.* First of all, we have to sort out the *vṛtti-s.* The *vṛtti-s* which are conducive to conjunction causing bondage have to be eradicated and the *vṛtti-s* which are conducive towards emancipation have to be adopted. And here lies the beauty of yoga.

CITTA – CONSCIOUSNESS

Let us see the thorny patch on which we have to use the 'yogic cutter' to remove and clear the thorns. One of the *Upaniṣada-s* say,

Mana eva manuṣyāṇām kāraṇam bandhaṁokṣayoh II

Man has been endowed with the greatest gift–the mind. However, most of the time this gift is not within our control. Instead of man utilising the mind, the mind utilises man. When the mind utilises us, we are in bondage and when we utilise the mind, we are liberated. The mind alone is the cause of bondage as well as liberation. This means that we have to learn how to use our mind thoughtfully and for that reason we need to know what the mind is.

Small children are introduced to kindergarten as a first step in learning. Similarly, for a man, the mind is his kindergarten or entrance to know the outer world or enter the inner world of his existence. The moment he begins to enter the inner world, he finds layer after layer, tier upon tier of the mind and he realises the unfathomable depth of the mind.

Water is the same everywhere, yet water on the surface of the ocean differs from that of the ocean's unfathomable depth as far as its appearance and flow is concerned. Similarly, the sky is the same everywhere, but we only know the sky above our head. The rest of the sky is a vast unknown space beyond our vision. In the same way, our inner body and inner mind too is as deep as the ocean and as vast as the sky.

The waves of the ocean are perceivable. Similarly, the mind, being at the surface and close to the body, it is perceivable like the waves of the ocean. On the surface of the mind only we are surfing. The mind fumbles with fugitive thoughts on account of unsteady and constant waving and wavering. It is as fickle or as shaky as a person trying to balance while surfing. It is like mercury which cannot be caught easily by hand. But if mercury is to be caught, then certain processing has to be carried out. Similarly, the mind, which is nearer to the body or the mind which is within our perceivable limits, has to be processed like mercury. This leads us to know the depth of the mind which stretches farther deep within the body.

As we begin to change the channel of the outer penetrating mind to interpenetrate, we begin to reach the subtlest and finest part of the mind, the consciousness or the *citta*. In other words, the mind or *manas* that discriminates is the gateway for us to reach the *citta*. This gives us an idea that the mind is just the outer layer of the *citta* functioning peripherally on the inner layer of the skin as a cognisable part of *citta* while the vast part of *citta* remains unknown, as the space in the sky remains unknown.

Citta, or consciousness, is a unique capsule, as the mind, ego or the I-maker and intellect are enclosed in it. All these components of *citta* are so closely inter-mingled and inter-related that it is hard to convey which overpowers which. The practice of yoga brings clarity in the modes of their behaviour and these components begin to show their modifications which are called *vṛtti-s,* or the waves of consciousness. As the direction of water can be traced on the ocean by the waves, so too the movements of *citta* can be traced by the *vṛtti-s. Vṛtti-s* indicate the movements of *citta.* The function, action, reaction, thinking, reasoning and reflecting are all movements of *citta* and these are expressed in the form of *vṛtti-s.*

To know more about the movements of consciousness, let us take the example of ourselves. We have noticed each man's nature and at the same time we have observed how each individual differs from another. We have seen how we ourselves behaved differently in our childhood than in our adolescence. A child behaves differently with his parents than with his teachers and his friends. At youth one is not the same as one is at middle age or at old age. As students, our behaviour differed when we grew up and matured. Marriage changes our attitude and parenthood changes our attitude even further. The profession that we choose brings changes within us. A school teacher has a different personality than that of a lawyer in court. But at the same time, the same teacher or lawyer will have a totally different attitude towards his own parents, wife, children and family than when he is not teaching at the school or arguing in court. The difference in attitude is marked according to one's approach to life. A scientist engrossed in his laboratory differs from that of a politician who is ambitious to have power. A religious person is more satisfied than a businessman, who wants to commercialise everything. A mature person differs from an immature person. Life's experience brings wisdom to some, whereas for others, the same experience may create mental problems.

I hope this clarifies the fact that man in his thinking, in his approach, in his action as well as in his attitude, behaviour, maturity and wisdom differs from another as well as in different situations and circumstances. One's reaction will not be the same all the time. That is why one person may be liked by someone and disliked by someone else. As a man can behave differently in different situations, the *citta* too can behave differently under different situations. As man attains maturity, he shows maturity in thinking. Similarly, the *citta*, shows maturity in right action and ways of thinking as the intellect begins to ripen.

I gave the example of you and me, since we often experience such things happening in ourselves. As *citta* is an instrument of man, its behaviour is the same. It is the *citta* which acts, reacts, interacts, behaves, remains blank or thinks in a thousand different ways and is pulled in a thousand different directions. Just as a pebble or a small stone is enough when dropped into the lake to create ripple after ripple, a single thought or object of thinking is enough to create several waves in the *citta*. A single thought can modify one's *citta*. That is how a baby goes to sleep while listening to lullabies. Seeing and listening is *pratyākṣa pramāṇa* – direct perception. If direct perception is one of the modifications of *citta*, sleep is another modification. These mental modifications or waves are called *vṛtti-s*. There are several *vṛtti-s* and they have been well classified and categorised.

VṚTTI-S – OBJECTIVE AND SUBJECTIVE

There are objective *vṛtti-s* and subjective *vṛtti-s*. The objective *vṛtti-s* are dependent upon external or outward factors and they are of two types, cognisable and non-cognisable. The subjective *vṛtti-s* are internal and are to be achieved and cultivated.

The objective *vṛtti-s* are *pramāṇa, viparyaya, vikalpa, nidrā* and *smṛti*. *Pramāṇa* is valid with direct knowledge. Knowledge that comes either by direct perception, correct inference or with proven words of wisdom is considered correct knowledge. *Viparyaya* is erroneous or perverted knowledge, *vikalpa* is imaginative thinking, *nidrā* is sleep and *smṛti* is memory.

All these five *vṛtti-s* are the channels or openings, the gates to gain knowledge. All our thinking processes and thought processes can be found in these channels of five types – the *vṛtti-s*. Nevertheless, as we change our thoughts and actions according to our maturity, the *vṛtti-s* too change. An out-going *vṛtti* expresses itself through the objective waves of the *citta*. The out-going *citta* earns the knowledge of the objective world.

But what about the in-coming thoughts of *citta*? The in-coming thoughts of *citta* are subjective waves. And these subjective waves, or subjective *vṛtti-s* of *citta* are the ones which have to be attended and achieved and are therefore, meritorious. It is meritorious and virtuous as the *citta* is tuned towards the core of the being. The in-coming waves of the *citta* gives knowledge of the subjective world. If the objective *vṛtti* is *vyutthān,a* the rest are subjective *vṛtti-s*. These are *nirodha, praśānta, ekāgra, nirmāṇa, chidra* and *divya*. Thus, *citta* in all has seven types of waves. It is the in-coming *vṛtti-s* that bring transformation and lead one towards the Self or the Soul.

The waves of the sea found at the sea shore differs from those in the middle of the ocean. The subjective waves are like the waves that are in the middle of the ocean. When one studies yoga, as an objective science or as an objective philosophy, the five objective *vṛtti-s (pramāṇa, viparyaya, vikalpa, nidrā* and *smṛti)* are helpful for categorising and understanding the mental modifications. But, when one practises yoga, then one has to know

Table 6. - The *vṛttis*

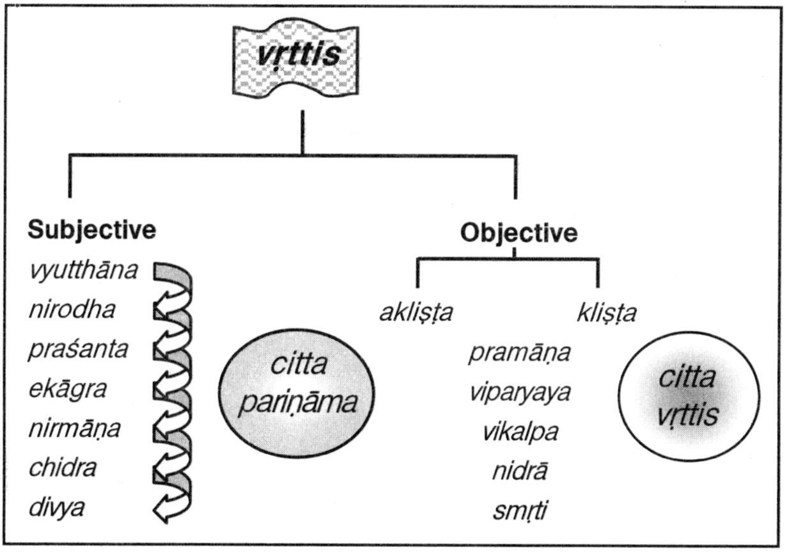

not only the subjective mental modifications, but the mental transformations also. This is known as *citta pariṇāma.* This *citta pariṇāma* leads one towards the root consciousness or *mūla citta,* which is as pure as the soul.

Well! It is better for you all to know the seven stages or states of transformations that the *citta* undergoes for the sake of involution in evolution of man.

The *vyutthāna citta* is the one from which thoughts emerge. If this *citta* is well organised, disciplined and capable of holding only to a single thought, then it leads one to march towards the soul.

Nirodha citta is where the consciousness restrains the rising or emerging thoughts. Between the rising thoughts and restraining thoughts, the consciousness experiences a calm and tranquil state. This is *praśānta citta.* Only in this tranquil state of consciousness one is able to develop a sharp one-pointed attention. This is *ekāgra citta.* As the seed sprouts to change into a tree, one-pointed consciousness – *ekāgra citta* – sprouts, cultivates and cultures as *nirmāṇa citta.* In this cultivated and refined consciousness, one has to check that loopholes are not left as imprints of past experiences, especially the defects such as ego or intellectual intoxication, intellectual pride (arrogance) and desire. The 'I' consciousness, which is very near to the self-consciousness can leave behind a fissure as *chidra citta* in the form of intellectual arrogance or pride. *Chidra* means fissure. Intellectual egoistic pride or intellectual intoxication is an obstacle in the path of *abhyāsa*. So are the desires too.

Desire or impression as *vāsanā* is a great obstacle in the path of *vairāgya*. Therefore, *abhyāsa* and *vairāgya* have to be followed in order to free the *citta* from pride, intoxication and desire, so that *citta* transforms into *divya* – pure, divine – *citta*. This is a divine state of *citta*, where it shines similar to the soul.

It will be interesting to note that when one is totally absorbed in practice, his mind is completely free from needs and greeds. Here what I mean to say is that if one is totally involved in *abhyāsa*, *vairāgya* follows. Hence yoga is like the two sides of the coin sticking together.

This is how and why one has to reach the depth with a full dimension of the *citta* by knowing its various layers.

Yoga is defined as restraint of the fluctuations of consciousness. Yoga brings the cessation of the movements in the consciousness.

Yogaḥ cittavṛtti nirodhaḥ // (*Y.S.*, I.2)

The *citta* has three functions; cognition, volition and motion. These three functions are not aimless. They are not mere waverings, flickerings or fluctuations. They occur to earn knowledge. Like a cloth, woven with threads, *citta* has five modifications namely correct knowledge, illusion, delusion, sleep and memory. This way *citta* is woven together with these five-fold modulations. Imagine a multi-coloured cloth which has several mixed coloured threads. The way these threads are arranged brings a totally different effect on the cloth. In the same way, we find our *citta* multi-coloured. Nevertheless, it disciplines itself with five modifications, not more and not less.

Now, know that the restraint of *citta* – *cittavṛtti nirodha* – is certainly not the suppression of *citta*. The modifications cannot be destroyed. They are made to fade away, but they do not fade easily. It is not easy to change one's behaviour, thoughts, attitude and opinions overnight. *Citta* requires its own time to change itself to the state of restraint. Discipline cannot be enforced. The more one forces the *citta*, it rebels, revolts and takes revenge. Therefore, one needs to handle, fondle and cajole the *citta* with great care and skill by organised discipline to check and restrain the modifications. Sometimes one has to rebuke and revise, revolutionise and revitalise the *citta* and its movements. With all these kinds of processing, the consciousness gets transformed from a fluctuating state to a stable state so that it reaches the highest state of emancipation.

In order to reach this state, one has to follow certain guidelines. These guidelines are called *ācāra-saṁhitā* and *vicāra-saṁhitā*. One has to follow a certain way of life and adopt a right way of thinking.

The objective *vṛtti-s* show the direction and enable us to channelise the thinking process. Therefore, the objective *vṛtti-s* are not arrested or restrained straight away. They are gradually transformed. It is exactly here that I draw a line between objective and subjective *vṛtti-s.*

The process of adopting right knowledge – *pramāṇa* and eradicating erroneous knowledge – *viparyaya,* filters and cleanses the thoughts and actions to a certain extent. Often the imagination also misleads our thoughts and actions. In fact, imagination – *vikalpa* – is the greatest gift for human beings. Instead of wasting it on fanciful thoughts, if one can direct ones highly imaginative power and apply that imaginative power to concepts such as the Supreme or God, it may guide one to march ahead on the spiritual path. For example, Patañjali defines God – *Īśvara* – as,

Kleśa karma vipāka āśayaiḥ aparāmṛṣṭaḥ puruṣaviśeṣaḥ Īśvaraḥ II (*Y.S.,* I.24)

God is a special unique entity – A Supreme Being – who is eternally free from conflicts and afflictions, unaffected by actions and untouched by cause and effect.

Ordinary people like us cannot think of such a Supreme Being who is not a personal God, who is not with form, shape or colour. We need to exert our power of imagination to structurise, visualise and perceive the God that is defined by Patañjali. Here, the objective *vṛtti* such as *vikalpa* is essential. But at the same time, we have to take care of ourselves and see that this *vikalpa* does not get modified into fantasy or fanciful thought. Otherwise, we will be lost in the mirage of a desert without finding God. The modification such as *vikalpa* defined by Patañjali has to be understood and realised through our *citta*. Therefore the *citta* has to undergo transformation. It is exactly at this stage that the objective *vṛtti-s* have to terminate and the subjective *vṛtti-s* have to sprout.

In order to save one from illusionary imaginations, the *nidrā-vṛtti* intelligises one to differentiate clearly between the state of *samādhi* and the state of sleep. Memory – *smṛti-vṛtti* is the accessory for all the *vṛtti-s* it links them and acts as a base making us aware of all the *vṛtti-s*. In this way the outgoing *vṛtti-s* guide the behaviour and thoughts for worldly knowledge or *laukika jñāna,* whereas the subjective *vṛtti-s* discipline, channel and refine them to move towards spiritual knowledge or *ādhyātmika jñāna*. The objective *vṛtti-s* are to be found in each and every one, as these mental modifications are common in all, irrespective of whether one practises yoga or not. But the subjective states of *citta* as explained earlier are traced only in the person who is a thorough practitioner of yoga. The true practitioner of yoga, firstly recognises and disciplines the objective *vṛtti-s*. These in turn, help him to curtail, chisel and shape the rightly chosen and cultured *vṛtti-s* in order to bring the transformation in *citta*. The quality of subjective *vṛtti-s* may differ according to the grade and standard of the practitioner who treads the path of yoga.

However, all these modified states of *citta,* whether objective or subjective are touched, tinged or polluted by *kleśa-s.* The *kleśa-s* pollute the *vṛtti-s* at every stage. In the objective modifications the *kleśa-s* come and interfere in a gross form, whereas, in the subjective flow of modifications they become subtle. It is a harder job to sort out the subtle afflictions than the gross afflictions. For this one needs a sharpened, sensitive intelligence.

KLEŚA-S – THE AFFLICTIONS

As there are five *vṛtti-s,* there are five *kleśa-s.* Let us see what *kleśa-s* are. *Kleśa-s* means afflictions which bring nothing but sorrow, pain and distress.

Kleśa-s are *avidyā, asmitā, rāga, dveṣa* and *abhiniveśa. Avidyā* is nescience or ignorance, *asmitā* is ego or pride, which may mislead even a learned person by creating a permanent impression that he is a realised soul, though he might not have reached that state. *Rāga* is affection and attachment towards pleasure and desires. *Dveṣa* is hatred and aversion towards the objects which bring unpleasant experiences. *Abhiniveśa* is an attachment towards life. It is very subtle but instinctive. It is the fear of death which can shake even the learned ones.

The *kleśa-s,* undoubtedly pollute the *vṛtti-s* and we must have experienced this very often. For instance, if we show anger at someone, then that anger changes our attitude into hatred. Then on, our each action and reaction towards that concerned person, may perhaps be unjust as the mind remains with that taint of anger. This is our day to day experience. Afflictions not only affect human beings but, also animals, though animals cannot express them verbally.

The gross afflictions are cognised quickly whereas the most subtle afflictions remain unknown or unfelt due to our insensitive intelligence. But the yoga *sādhanā* develops in the *sādhaka* this sensitive intelligence on his onward yogic journey.

We have in us channels of action – *karma nāḍī* – and channels of knowledge – *jñāna nāḍi.* We do not easily understand how one affects the other. Our *karma-s* or our actions, depend upon our *jñāna* or knowledge and again the knowledge that we

Table 7. - Afflictions and Modifications

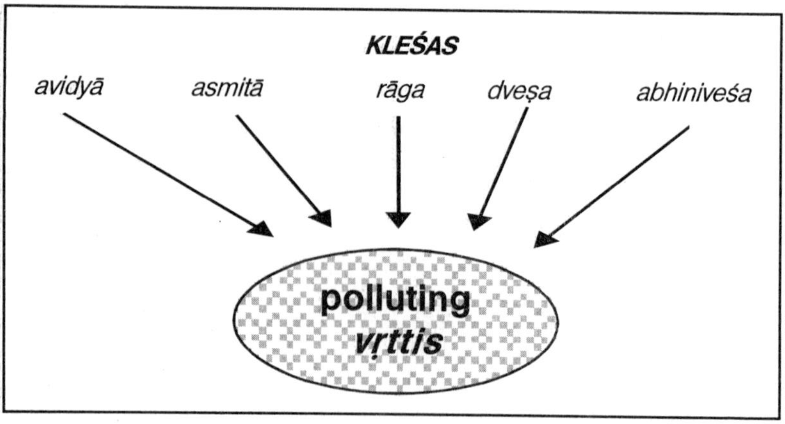

acquire depends upon *karma*. If *ācāra* or the practical approaches are rooted in *kleśa-s* then *vicāra* – or the discriminative thinking processes are rooted in *vṛtti-s*. Therefore, it is very hard for a common man to find out whether *ācāra* is affecting *vicāra* or *vicāra* is affecting *ācāra*. However, if the practitioner of yoga is sensitive, this clarity certainly occurs to him and therefore he is able to have *karma-śuddhi* and *jñāna-śuddhi*, as well as *ācāra-śuddhi* and *vicāra-śuddhi* which leads him soon towards *citta-śuddhi*. *Śuddhi* means purification. When both action and knowledge are purified, then behaviour and thoughts also are purified, leading towards the purification of consciousness.

Now, as far as the practitioner of yoga is concerned, the *sādhaka* has to purify his actions and thoughts. However, it is not the gross afflictions that bother him as he can eradicate the gross afflictions with *sādhanā*. The gross afflictions affect the objective *vṛtti-s*, but the subtle, hidden or latent afflictions affect the subjective *vṛtti-s*. The subtle afflictions are unknown to the gross outer mind. The outer mind cannot catch the subtle afflictions. The outer layer of the mind is less sensitive to subtle afflictions, whereas the *citta* is very sensitive to subtle afflictions.

When a practitioner begins his inner journey from the *vyutthāna* to *nirodha* state or from *nirodha* to *praśānta* and journeys towards *divya citta*, his sharp sensitivity cannot miss even the subtlest affliction. This botheration is very subtle, sharp and intense. For this, I can sight an example. Have we not experienced the sensitivity of our eyes which cannot bear even the minutest dust particle touching or entering in? Our eyes blink and begin to water immediately. We are keen to protect our eyes and quick to remove the dust. Similarly, the subtle afflictions that bother the *citta* react at once and put a brake on the modifications for it to move and reach the final aims of yoga, namely, liberation from bondage.

Let me take your attention a little more towards the modifications of *citta*. We saw the five objective and subjective modifications of *citta*. These five *vṛtti-s* express themselves in two ways. These *vṛtti-s* can be painful and non-painful, *kliṣṭa* or *akliṣṭa*. The *kleśa-s* – the afflictions, are always painful and tangible whereas the *vṛtti-s* are obscure. One cannot draw a line between *kliṣṭa* and *akliṣṭa-vṛtti*. Often what we think of as *akliṣṭa-vṛtti* or non-painful mental modification may prove to be *kliṣṭa-vṛtti* or painful modification. They are very subtle in their expression. It is like mistaking deep sleep – *nidrā-vṛtti* – for *samādhi*. One may be doing *dhyāna* and at a point the *dhyāna* may end up in sleep. A deep sleepy state in *Śavāsana* can be mistaken for *samādhi*. In *nidrā-vṛtti*, the *citta* witnesses nothing. This void state cannot be mistaken for the positive state of witnessing the soul. These mistakes occur on account of one of the afflictions, that is *avidyā*.

One may sit for meditation and go to a sleepy or dreamy state. This mental modification should not be considered as meditation. Similarly, in the *vikalpa vṛtti*, the concept of soul or the union between *jīvātman* and *paramātman*, may remain a fanciful idea as long as one does not experience the feel of the soul or the union of *jīvātman* with *paramātman*. Even high imaginative capacities can prove to be ineffective and sometimes end up in mental imbalances.

Viparyaya is another *vṛtti* which means a mistaken or perverted identity and this always ends in *kliṣṭa-vṛtti* – a painful modification. *Viparyaya* is the biggest hurdle in the path of knowledge. The *viparyaya* – wrong perception – can be corrected only by *pramāṇa* – valid and experienced knowledge. By re-examination, *viparyaya vṛtti* is corrected to experience its *akliṣṭa* phase.

Valid knowledge is gained either through direct perception, inference or reference to authoritative scriptures and testimonials of experienced wise people. It is true that *viparyaya* can be corrected through *pramāṇa,* but at the same time *pramāṇa* also needs to be scrutinised. For instance, water is colourless, but it seems as though it has colour since it looks blue due to the reflection of the blue sky. And again, the sky is colourless, but our eyes witness the blue colour through our direct perception. Therefore, children cannot be considered wrong if they say that the sky is blue. Water seems to be green because of green moss and red when there is red mud in it. But science proves that the water is neither red nor green nor blue. Our eyes witness the colour but the eyes of science deny what we are witnessing. Therefore, one cannot hold the validity of the senses as always correct. The *pramāṇa vṛtti* is also a subject for verification. It is knowledge coming through our direct perception. It is in our hands to make use of it correctly. The knowledge has to be verified by the intellect and yoga teaches the way to sharpen the intellect. I will be dealing with this aspect a little later. This way all the five *vṛtti-s* have mixed *kliṣṭa* and *akliṣṭa* phases.

If we have to direct the energy of *citta* towards the soul, we need to study the *vṛtti-s*, verify them and correct their flow. This can be done only with *abhyāsa*. First we need to study and understand the *citta* and its *vṛtti-s* before we restrain them. We also need to cultivate *vairāgya* for this restraint. So, firmly hold the ropes of *abhyāsa* and *vairāgya* to climb to the peak of emancipation and liberation from wants.

To be honest, when the practitioner of yoga has earned the exalted state of intelligence or *vivekaja jñāna*, then his consciousness reaches the state of mature wisdom with insight *"ṛtaṁbharā tatra prajñā II"* (*Y.S.*, I.48). From then on he does only non-painful actions as he experiences the end of all afflictions that accrue from actions. See *tataḥ kleśa karma nivṛttiḥ II* (*Y.S.*, IV.30).

ANTARĀYA-S – THE OBSTACLES

Now, let us see how the *antarāya-s* – the obstacles, come in our way, what their conditions are and how to conquer them.

Modern medical science says that the so-called diseases are psychosomatic. Psyche is mind and soma is body. The diseases enter in and express themselves through the body and affect the mind. When the diseases begin to affect the body, the mind recognises that something is wrong in the body. But we don't know that the disease has affected the mind first before the body. This is because we are less sensitive to recognise when it has touched the mind. It may send signals, but we cannot hear or we do not listen or sense to listen. Our ego comes in the way and does not admit or accept this fact. Like trains that get shunted, the ego too shunts and changes its way of thinking and denies that there is an ailment though the body is affected. This may be due to arrogance or heedlessness in oneself.

Even medical science finds the cause of disease outside the body. But the actual disturbance occurs within the body. Among the three qualities or the three constituents of nature or *prakṛti,* namely, *sattva, rajas* and *tamas,* the latter two cause the disease. When *rajas* and *tamas* are contaminated by *ahaṁkāra,* disease sets in. But *ahaṁkāra* does not admit that easily. *Rajas* and *tamas* begin to further contaminate the mind and body with the pastures of pleasures.

One can find two remedies, either to accept and live with it or minimise and eradicate the disease. This is done through the introduction of medicine or through sheer willpower, using one's inner defensive power to combat the disease. If a diseased person loses his willpower then he succumbs to the disease. Hence,it is certainly a matter of application of the willpower to overcome disease. At the same time, one cannot forget that the disease enters through the same mind that lacked willpower.

Lord Krishna, cautions us in the *Bhagavad Gītā,* that we should be well disciplined and regulate our food habits, sleep and movements in daily life. We have to plan the programme in such a way that the body and mind do not get unnecessarily exhausted. Pride or *ahaṁkāra* sometimes misleads and enforces one to go beyond one's capacity. So both body and mind have to be regulated to work in concordance. Otherwise, they may cause imbalance creating uneasiness in body and mind. Also, one should be aware that uneasiness in body and mind weakens the willpower. A strong will burns like fire. This is called *preraṇā-śakti.*

Preraṇā means a driving force or an incitement. Incitement is the very life force of *prakṛti.* This driving force enters the body along with the self at the time of birth. *Āyurveda* says that this force establishes itself in the *kāraṇa śarīra* – the causal body – along with the soul in the mother's womb. It incites, provokes and instigates life in one and burns like fire, oozing out willpower and desire. Do not mistake this force for the ego. *Preraṇā* is the inducing power in one's self, whereas ego is the component of consciousness, the *citta.* When the dark clouds of ego shade the initiating power, or driving force – *preraṇā,* it does not take time for the thunderbolt of *bhoga* to pour the rain of *roga* – diseases – to afflict one.

When we say that one needs strong nerves, willpower and determined hope to fight and overcome disease and suffering, there is truth in it. Otherwise the disease swallows the sufferer and makes him succumb to it.

Patañjali might have not used the word *preraṇā*, but he has certainly indicated what it means. In *"Sa tu dīrghakāla nairantarya satkāra āsevitaḥ dṛḍhabhūmiḥ II"* (*Y.S.*, I.14), Patañjali wants the devotees of yoga to be *tīvrasaṁvegins* with *vīrya* – valour and *śraddhā* – determined intent. Hence, a highly intense practitioner or aspirant – a *tīvrasaṁvegin* – needs a high potential full of confidence, vigour, tremendous memory power and attentive awareness.

The subject of yoga, as a curative science, has always remained a topic for debate. But Patañjali certainly has made us aware of the fact that the diseases are psycho-somatic. Their root cause is in the 'ego' and one needs to develop willpower to understand the cause in order to get free from disease and suffering.

Patañjali, in *Samādhi Pāda*, lists hordes of diseases. Some diseases and their causes are referred to in medical books and some which are very subtle cannot be found in these.

A common man understands that, that which brings discomfort to the body and uneasiness to the mind, is disease.

Conventional medical science does not accept yoga as a curative science, as the diseases are not treated by their method of administration of medicines. Yoga treats disease by tapping the body's defence force by willpower. I feel that this misunderstanding may be partly due to a want of knowledge of present day teachers for its value in prevention and cure of disease. There are also some, who belittle yoga as a type of contortion. I feel that these misunderstandings arise partly on account of ignorance and partly on account of pride. When I say partly, I mean that some could be really ignorant and innocent of the depth of yoga, while others are proud of their knowledge and therefore don't want to go to a deeper study of yogic science.

Patañjali knows very well how the common man gets afflicted by disease and how he can be cured through yoga. For this reason alone, he refers to *vyādhi* – disease of the body and mind – as the first obstacle. As I said earlier, a yogi is highly sensitive to the subtlest afflictions; whereas a common man is sensitive to the physical diseases. He wants to get rid of the physical uneasiness first. Therefore, the practice of *āsana* becomes essential for him to get rid of the problems. That is why a common man adopts the practice of *āsana-s* in his *sādhanā*. For this, one cannot criticise yoga as being a set of contortions with no bearing on prevention or cure. The prevention and curing aspect of yoga is one branch in the totality of yoga. If the *sādhaka* limits his *sādhanā* to this level and does not proceed further to feel the depth of the subject, then this is not the fault of the hidden wisdom of yoga, but of the practitioner.

However, Patañjali makes the practitioner aware of the depth of the subject as well as the depth of the obstacles so that the doer understands how much effort is needed to have a healthy body, a healthy mind and a healthy self. Correcting the obstacles that appear at the very beginning is prevention and tracing the cause and striking the disease at the root itself is the cure.

Patañjali makes us aware of the diseases when he introduces us to the functions and activities of our *citta*. *Citta* gets modified so rapidly that before we recognise one *vṛtti* and verify it, it gets muddled into another. These muddled changes are a natural process in many of us. They show the aliveness of the *citta*. All our activities depend upon the mental modifications and modulations. Even a common man who is not a practitioner of yoga, can notice these. As the doctor checks the pulse and heart beats to see whether the patient is alive or not, a practitioner of yoga essentially listens to the movements of *citta* to find out whether it is alive positively or has sunk into negativity.

The doctor diagnoses the physical and physiological disease of the patient, whereas a yoga *sādhaka* has to diagnose the disease of the *citta* – the mind, intelligence and ego also.

Suppose the *citta's* fluctuations are defectively modified, can these not be considered as diseases? Have we not noticed mentally deranged patients who do not have right perception? Do we not sometimes mistake a rope as a snake and get frightened? The deranged man may express his debility in public, but you and I toss inside just like an insane person. How often do we indulge in erroneous knowledge and never heed and correct ourselves. As long as *avidyā* is there, *viparyaya* will also be there. Ignorance and erroneous knowledge are not far from each other.

Those who do not come out from the imaginative thoughts – *vikalpa* – never command respect. Similarly, though sleep recuperates and rejuvenates man, it can be defective also. Those who experience a healthy, peaceful sleep are the blessed ones whereas those with dreams, who suffer from insomnia, fear, fatigue and restlessness, live in discomfort. A perfect memory is very good. We appreciate those who have an extraordinary memory, but what about those who have a defective memory or those who repeatedly remember something bad like the hysterical patient? The *sādhaka* uses discrimination to sort out the wanted memory from the unwanted memory, but a deranged person cannot use discrimination and therefore, continues to store and cherish wrong memories.

I point out these defects because in my seventy-two years of teaching, I have come across people who were highly educated, well studied, philosophers and yoga practitioners, but showed such defects.

Well! Those who have gone wrong in their approach, experience all the defective mental modifications. An erroneous practice of yoga can make *vṛtti-s* get deranged. Therefore, it is the responsibility of the *sādhaka-s* to see, before restraining the *vṛtti-s,* so that they organise the *vṛtti-s* which do not develop such defects.

Devotion and dedication are the most essential qualities required in any field. A similar devotion and dedication is needed in yoga if one has to progress, either in *preyas* – the worldly pleasures and joys, or *śreyas* – the spiritual endeavour and emancipation. When the dedication and devotion is towards God then it is recognised as *bhakti*.

Patañjali puts it in a beautiful way. He does not believe in blind devotion. He certainly does not say, "Have *bhakti* and do nothing". He introduces effortful *bhakti*. It is very important to know how he has sequentially made an approach towards devotion.

First of all, to reach towards the highest *nirbīja samādhi*, he demands *śraddhā* – faith, trust and confidence. But he does not accept mere faith. He wants vigour and valour to go with it. *Śraddhā* is an offspring of *vīrya*. Faith comes after revelation and then one faithfully gets attached to the object or ideal and detached from all other things. This is *vairāgya* in *vīryatā*. *Vīrya* – vigour or valour is dependent on *abhyāsa*. It is developed with constant practise. However, *smṛti* – memory and *samādhi prajñā* – total awareness in contemplation, contain both *abhyāsa* and *vairāgya*. One has to have a meaningful memory in order to support and allow one to continue the *sādhanā*. This memory is developed through *abhyāsa*. There are certain memories which have to be erased and those can only be erased by *vairāgya*. Similarly, in contemplation, *abhyāsa* and *vairāgya* remain balanced.

Having faith, vigour, memory and attentive contemplation, the practitioner has to be supremely vigorous and intense in practice. Patañjali, having a soft corner for his *sādhaka-s* who may not be able to be intense, accepts their mild or medium approaches, but at the same time asks them to strengthen themselves by praying, contemplating and surrendering to God. This method is meant to develop *vairāgya*. Patañjali defines and explains the method of praying to God and the fruition or result occurring. At this point, he lists the impediments and says that in order to prevent the impediments one should have a single-minded effort. This is again *abhyāsa*. This kind of emphasis proves that *abhyāsa* and *vairāgya* are essential to restrain the mental modifications and to overcome the impediments as well. Patañjali does not believe that the impediments can be eradicated by just praising God – *Īśvara prāṇidhāna*. Effort is also needed. Let us see these impediments or obstacles that fluctuate the *citta*.

Vyādhi styāna saṁśaya pramāda ālasya avirati bhrāntidarśana alabdhabhūmikatva anavasthitatvāni cittavikṣepaḥ te antarāyāḥ // (*Y.S.*, I.30) and

Duḥkha daurmanasya aṅgamejayatva śvāsapraśvāsāḥ vikṣepa sahabhuvaḥ // (*Y.S.*, I.31).

It means that the obstacles are disease, inertia, doubt, heedlessness, laziness, indiscipline of the senses, erroneous views, lack of perseverance and backsliding. Along with them comes sorrow, despair, unsteadiness of the body and irregular breathing, which distract the *citta* further. Or it can be presumed that the symptoms of all diseases are expressed through fear, grief, pain, instability in body and laboured breathing.

Table 8. - The *Antarāyas* — The Obstacles

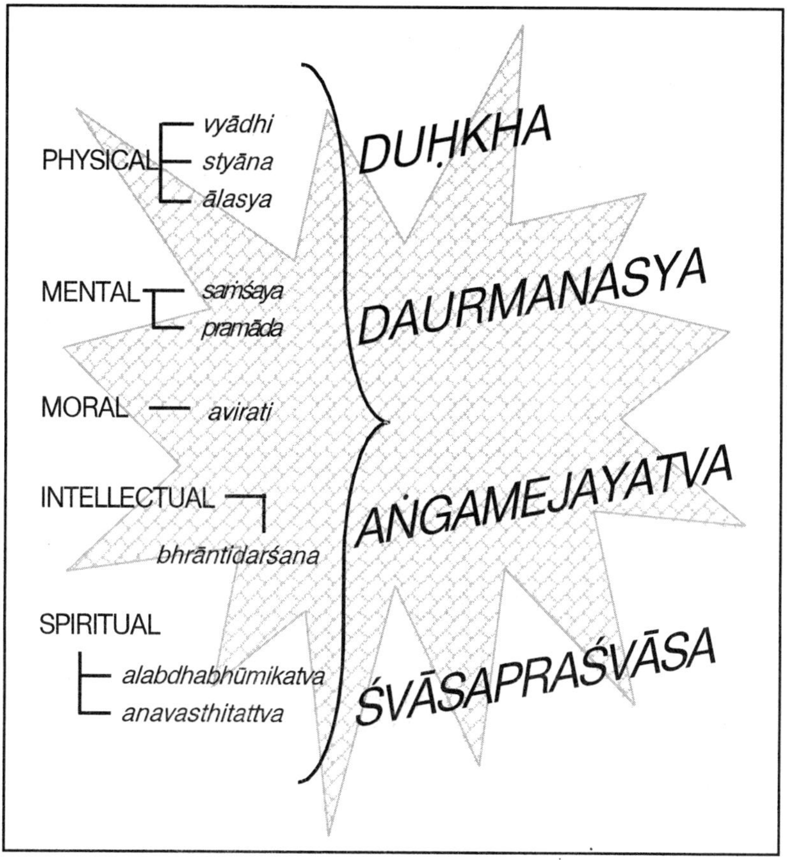

Vyādhi means disease. It may be physical, physiological, psychological, emotional, mental or intellectual. *Styāna* means mental laziness as well as sluggishness. It comes due to a lack of interest, leading one to have a casual approach. Such people are good at preaching, but they do not follow what they preach. *Saṁśaya* means doubt. This doubt occurs because of lack of faith. Sometimes 'to doubt' is right but it should be constructive to march forwards and not destructive pulling one down and leading towards indecision. *Pramāda* means carelessness. It is where one lacks the feeling of responsibility and therefore, becomes heedless. This heedlessness is sheer negligence on one's part. Pride-intoxicated people become careless. Success goes to their head and it becomes a disease.

Ālasya is physical laziness. Lazy people speak a lot but do nothing. They need to be taught 'facta non verba'. *Avirati* means lack of control. We often say that we are interested in a subject, but at the same time we are so fickle minded that we run after some other subject, proving that we are 'Jack of all trades and master of none'. *Bhrāntidarśana* means living under an illusion. This again is a disease of imagination. It is a kind of fantasy. If day dreaming is a behavioural or psychic disease, then illusion or mistaken notion is an intellectual disease. Then comes *alabdhabhūmikatva,* which means the inability to hold on to what is achieved. This is a spiritual disease causing emotional disturbance. A *sādhaka* misses the bus here. This leads towards anxiety and oscillation called *anavasthitattva,* or spiritual retardation.

All these impediments, whether physical or moral, mental or emotional, intellectual or spiritual, cover the body and mind expressing themselves as sorrowful or depressive states of mind, bringing unsteadiness in the body and un-rhythmic, defective, laboured and shallow breathing. Finally the body, the mind and the breath are all affected. The vital energy gets sapped and the *sādhaka* snaps.

All these impediments not only scatter and oscillate the *citta* but they shake the body, depress the mind, misguide the senses, stagnate the intelligence, inflate the ego and darken the consciousness, blocking the healthy state of the *sādhaka*. Then, the *sādhaka* as a seer gets identified with the seen and forgets his own true nature.

THE HEALING *VṚTTI-S*

We have seen that Patañjali does not accept *bhakti* without efforts. To overcome these obstacles and impediments, we have to practise and this is *abhyāsa*. Patañjali introduces *abhyāsa* as a single-minded effort for transforming the *citta* towards favourable modulations. One has to embellish *citta*, so that the *vṛtti-s* are channelled in the right direction for a healthy contented life flow. For this one has to develop certain constructive, positive *vṛtti-s* of the life force and discard negative and destructive *vṛtti-s*.

What are those constructive *vṛtti-s* which we have to develop? They are *maitrī vṛtti* – friendliness, *karuṇā vṛtti* – compassion, *muditā vṛtti* – gladness, *upekśā vṛtti* – indifference, *prāṇa vidhāraṇa vṛtti* – restraining of *prāṇa, manasa stithi nibandhanī vṛtti II* (*Y.S.*, I.35) – contemplation upon an object that is conducive to bring steadiness in mind, *viśokā vṛtti* – cultivating a sorrowless state of mind through *jyotiṣmati vṛtti* (*Y.S.*, I.36) – absorbed in the contemplation of the luminosity of saints and *yogi-s*. According to Patañjali, these *vṛtti-s* are an alternative method to bring mental equilibrium in the sufferer.

Why do I say that you have to cultivate these mental *vṛtti-s?* Because the objective *vṛtti-s* are related to the external world and they scatter and confuse the internal mind. Such *vṛtti-s* have to be combed, investigated, sifted and filtered. In the beginning these processes may appear complicated, but by disciplined effort one can train these *vṛtti-s* to bring *citta prasādanam* – grace and equilibrium – in the consciousness. *Citta prasādanam* is the gateway to enter the spiritual kingdom (*Y.S.,* I.33).

Let us take the first constructive *vṛtti* – *maitrī-vṛtti. Maitrī* means friendliness. It also means to be happy and comfortable in life. This does not mean that we should open a 'friends club'. A friends club may lead to entanglements. As practitioners of yoga, we should not allow our *citta* to get tainted with hate, avarice or revenge. We must not hate or show animosity or develop avarice towards a person or his belongings because we do not possess them. Negative feelings and thoughts develop out of sorrowful and disturbing situations which get further shattered. The perception of someone else's happiness can vitiate one's mind. Therefore, we have to develop friendliness in order to be free from enmity. We should not be an enemy or a foe towards such happy people. We have to cultivate friendliness in ourselves and accept their happiness as their good luck and not show unfriendliness or malice towards them. Learning to be friendly is more important than friendship. Friendliness is attached to our emotional state, whereas friendship is just a law of social intercourse.

Similarly, compassion or *karuṇā*. Compassion is a dynamic sympathy to show towards those who are in sorrow, or gladness – *muditā* – towards those who are better placed or are more virtuous than us. This way the *yoga-sādhaka* has to change his attitude. One has to alter one's entire thinking and thought processes.

Upekṣā is indifference. This indifference is to be cultivated first within himself, by not paying attention to good and bad, pleasure and pain, and then shown towards those who do not heed the right guideline, given repeatedly to change their ways of seeing and living. Friendliness, compassion and gladness need a positive approach through *abhyāsa*, whereas indifference has to be built by the quality of measured *vairāgya*.

"maitrī karuṇā muditā upekṣāṇāṁ sukha duḥkha puṇya apuṇya viṣayāṇāṁ bhāvanātaḥ cittaprasādanam II" (*Y.S.*, I.33).

As friendliness, compassion, gladness and judicial indifference create right moods and thought waves, so does the breathing process. Hence Patañjali suggests,

Pracchardana vidhāraṇābhyāṁ vā prāṇasya II (*Y.S.*, I.34)

It means, to maintain the pensive state felt at the time of soft, steady exhalation and passive retention after exhalation. This quiet, serene state of consciousness can be felt by all during *kuṁbhaka* after exhalation. This is called *bāhya kuṁbhaka*.

The smooth flow of exhalation itself is exhilarating and soothing. The pensive state of mind is brought about by soft and steady exhalation. The passive retention followed after exhalation soothes the nerves and quietens the breath and mind and in turn puts a brake to the *vṛtti-s.* We may be engulfed in a sorrowful state, but the very core or inner heart is sorrowless. This is the seat of the soul. Reach this very source through slow, 'echo exhalation' and you will be amazed to experience the *vṛtti-s* getting silenced. The echo exhalation is the final silent exhalation that continues once the normal exhalation is over. The same experience occurs in a concert hall where the sound of the last notes played by the performers on their instruments merges into the hall echoing and re-echoing. This experience is hearing the minutest silence in silence. Silence in echo exhalation is reached with careful observation and reflection on the inner vibration and sound that fades out gradually in exhalation. Once the audible exhalation ceases and reaches the inaudible state, it is *citta prasādanam.*

Tranquillity is disturbed if the breath goes wrong. The mind wavers and *vṛtti-s* develop which do not allow one to reach the core of the being. Of course steadfastness cannot come like magic in a day. One requires *abhyāsa* – effortful practice. One requires *anuśāsanam* or discipline followed by *guru paraṁparā* of yoga. One requires knowledge of the aim of yoga. One requires guidance in yoga and the discipline of yoga. One requires *anuṣṭhāna* of yoga – a devoted and religious practice of yoga. One requires *ekatattvābhyāsa* – practice with single-minded effort.

We saw how man becomes diseased. Nobody really is at ease. Ease has to be achieved through practice. We saw how the *vṛtti-s* which are the gateways to knowledge, indirectly bring disease. We saw the *antarāya-s* – the obstacles that vitiate and contaminate man ranging from the physical to the spiritual diseases. Fortunately, Patañjali gives remedial measures. He is not only consoling and encouraging us, but leading us towards the path of yoga.

We saw how Patañjali explains the diseases and remedial measures in *Samādhi Pāda*. In the *Sādhana Pāda* he brings our attention to the causes of disease, the *kleśa-s* – the afflictions, *duḥkha* – the sorrows and *vitarka bādhana* – obstructive doubt.

Patañjali explains that the root cause of the disease is not outside but inside us in the form of ignorance, pride, desire, abhorrence and attachments which inflict sorrows and he says that these can be reduced or vanquished through the practice of yoga. The attenuation of an affliction is a remedy. The word for remedy is practice. As practice is full of action, it is called *'kriyā'* and the discipline of yoga is *'kriyā yoga'.* Patañjali mentions *kriyā yoga* in the form of *tapas* – zealous action, *svādhyāya* – knowledge and wisdom and *Īśvara praṇidhāna* – humbleness and surrender of oneself to the Supreme Universal Soul. In short he speaks of work, word and wisdom. These have to be adopted and adapted practically according to the conditions of body, mind and self.

Tapas is an orderly discipline to get rid of *tāpa-s* – afflictions, or cause of grievousness. *Svādhyāya* is the study of ones own body, mind and self and *Īśvara praṇidhāna* is devotion to God to develop freedom from ego consciousness. This threefold *kriyā yoga* covers all the eight aspects of *aṣṭāṅga yoga.*

Before drawing your attention to *kriyā yoga,* hidden in the eight aspects of yoga, let us consider *duḥkha* and *vitarka bādhana,* which are necessary to be known before we search for remedies.

No doubt, these days yoga has become a very popular subject, and has gained ground for its remedial values.

Man is a pleasure-seeking animal. With his high thinking power he does not know when he falls a prey to the pleasures. Nobody wants pain. Nobody wants suffering. Nobody wants diseases. Yet one does not realise that sorrow is implicit in pleasures. Each and every being wants to be happy. But unfortunately, getting caught in the enjoyment of the pleasures, one gets hooked into the chain of sorrow. Suppose you have the gift of good health in body and mind and if you utilise this in a right manner without amusing or abusing this gift, it helps you. But if you amuse and abuse this good health, then certainly you end up in pain.

Similarly, wealth is a need. Wealth is a need for one's living. There is nothing wrong if one wants to live happily and comfortably. If wealth is misused you end up in sorrow. There is no end to pleasure, temptation and happiness, they are like adding fuel to the fire. When pleasures are not fulfilled and when the temptations are not satisfying, real happiness cannot be experienced.

We say that each black cloud has a silver lining. This silver lining may be a solace to us and a hope when we are in a hopeless state of suffering. Once the suffering is over, we forget everything. Because of attachment to happiness the clouds of sorrow may appear again. Therefore, practice of yoga makes a man learn to be contented rather than hunting after pleasures. Contentment does not come easily without the tinge of *vairāgya* or desirelessness and passionlessness. This is why Patañjali points out that *viveka* without *vairāgya* is valueless. The discriminative discernment, minus desirelessness, is of no use.

Man loses his contentment while searching for pleasure. Therefore he loses happiness too. Pleasure is like alcohol. Once you get addicted to pleasure, de-addiction is time consuming. The de-addiction process requires a tremendous willpower as the root of sorrow is in the pleasure-seeking mind and by willpower one has to tame the mind.

The sources for sorrows are of three types. These are *pariṇāma duḥkha, tāpa duḥkha* and *saṁskāra duḥkha.* While seeking pleasures, we don't know when we get entangled and become addicted to them. We enjoy the pleasures and the moment we miss them or lose them, we are in sorrow. The craving for pleasure is never ending.

Because of want of satisfaction, the pleasure-giving objects finally bring pain and sorrow. This type of sorrow is called *pariṇāma duḥkha.* This discontentment with pleasure ultimately changes into pain. *Pariṇāma* means change or result. Pain is the result of pleasure. This hankering after pleasure is a kind of disease, like addiction.

The next is *tāpa duḥkha. Tāpa* means torment, pain, sorrow, distress or anxiety. Basically it conveys the meaning of burning with heat or fire. The attachment to pleasures bring *pariṇāma duḥkha* and aversion to pains bring *tāpa duḥkha.* In *tāpa duḥkha,* we miss what we want to have. We hate those who have what we do not have. We compare ourselves with others and therefore we do not enjoy what we have. You cannot disguise the aversion within yourself since it shows the burning sorrow outside. This not only causes physical disease but also psychological disease. *Tāpa* creates a mental dearth.

The third is called *saṁskāra duḥkha. Saṁskāra* means latent imprints. Whether pleasure or pain, attachment or aversion, wishes fulfilled or unfulfilled, objects enjoyed or not enjoyed, all these experiences leave imprints deep in the heart. They cannot be easily washed off. Even the memory of such experiences remains deep rooted, causing pain. The *saṁskāra duḥkha* is there from time immemorial, adding new imprints to the old ones. Therefore, I said at the beginning alone that yoga is meant to control and restrain the latent or subliminal impression, *Yogaḥ saṁskāravṛtti nirodhaḥ* *//*,. All these types of *duḥkha* whether *pariṇāma duḥkha* or *tāpa duḥkha* or *saṁskāra duḥkha,* are within our experiential world. They are cognisable.

As a matter of fact, all these *duḥkha-s* are hidden and latent in the *guṇa-s,* or the qualities of nature, which are quite contrary to each other. These *guṇa-s* or qualities are *sattva, rajas* and *tamas,* which function as illumination, activity and inertia. If one brings placidity, the second brings turbulence and the third delusion. These three *guṇa-s* suppress each other, dominate each other and disturb each other. They dash against each other. They act, react and interact. They bring mixed pleasure and pain as well as delusion.

All these *duḥkha-s* or sorrows, rotate in such a manner that we do not know which one we are facing. Therefore, the pain remains as pain and the sorrow remains as sorrow. Patañjali asks us to analyse, distinguish and sort out the *duḥkha-s* so that we touch the root cause and practise yoga accordingly. As practitioners of yoga we have developed a little bit of *'viveka'* – discrimination. Hence, it is possible for us to learn, analyse and trace the root cause of sorrow that lies in the *guṇa-s* through our *viveka* or discriminative power in order to bring balance in our minds.

After explaining the *pariṇāma duḥkha, tāpa duḥkha* and *saṁskāra duḥkha,* the functioning of the *guṇa-s,* the *vṛtti-s* (constructive as well as destructive) and the *antarāya-s,* let us see how the principles of yoga, as the silver lining of the dark clouds of obstructions keep us to release ourselves from the clutches of the negative forces of health and life.

Aṣṭāṅga yoga makes the intelligence *(buddhi),* or the element of *vāyu,* to reach the remotest part of the body of the *sādhaka,* so that the consciousness *(citta),* or the element of ether, leads the seer *(ātman)* to envelope the body. Here, the difference between the seen, body, and the seer *(ātman)* disappears and they associate as one. This is the silver lining of man through yoga.

Thus, *aṣṭāṅga yoga* builds up in the doer the health of the body, clarity of the mind and contentment of the self to make him shine and show reverence for life as well as towards one and all.

Before explaining the application of the principles of yoga, let us study and understand the functioning of the *guṇa-s* by first going through the two most important principles of yoga namely *yama* and *niyama* which I will explain in brief as I elaborate on them later.

As the *guṇa-s* vibrate, so too does the *citta.* Similarly, *citta* fluctuates as the *guṇa-s* fluctuate. The *guṇa-s* dominate each other to prove their predominance and it is the same with *citta.*

You don't know how much power, how much strength and how much potency the principles of *yama* and *niyama* have in order to channel the *guṇa-s!* Therefore, I say that *yama* and *niyama* are meant for *guṇa-vṛtti nirodha* – restraint of *guṇa-vrtti*. The principles of *yama* shine with *sattva guṇa*. But *tamas* darkens these principles and we begin to oppose them. We disobey the rules when *tamas* dominates us. The principles of *niyama* activate us and energise us to follow the principles of *yama*. By following the five principles of *yama* and five principles of *niyama*, we are able to check the undisciplined movements, as well as the unanticipated action and reaction of *sattva*, *rajas* and *tamas*. The two aspects of *yama* and *niyama* save us from falling into the valley of sorrow.

Yama and *niyama* are the ethical or moral foundations which are essential in the practice of yoga. Often people criticise me, saying that I am merely a practitioner of *āsana* and *prāṇāyāma*. They think that I am not teaching *yama* and *niyama*. Know very well that without moral discipline, the gateway to spiritual experience is out of question. It can be taught objectively by a lecture or by information but it will not have any imprint on the listener. But I make you to follow the ethical principles moment to moment without using these words. I teach subjectively to follow *yama* and *niyama* in *āsana* and *prāṇāyāma* to change yourself from the very core.

One has to sink within to refine ones character, ones behaviour, ones attitude and ones way of thinking and acting. I build up the inner character of the practitioner through *āsana-s* and *prāṇāyāma-s* which teaches them to follow *yama* and *niyama.*

Yama and *niyama* are the pillars of righteousness - *dharma.* However, unrighteousness and indiscipline - *adharma* - cannot be easily uprooted. *Yama* and *niyama* are the potential seeds of the spiritual tree. By mere mention of the importance of *yama* and *niyama,* nobody can become adepts in ethical and moral disciplines. They are hard to follow as the mind is caught in the web of '*vitarka bādhana*'. *Vitarka* means thinking. *Bādhana* means trouble or obstruction. This clearly shows the defective thinking process.

"I think, therefore I am". "I doubt, therefore I am". So said Descartes. The thinking proves our existence. The greatest gift man has is the power of thinking and we all welcome this power. But when we wrongly make use or abuse this power, it becomes *vitarka bādhana. Vitarka bādhana* is a disease of dubious thinking which comes to distract us from following *yama* and *niyama.* To overcome *vitarka bādhana* we need to correct our thoughts and actions by righteous and rational thoughts to act in a rightful healthy way.

When we want to observe *yama* and *niyama,* we become like children. Our minds will be like that of a child at that time. The child wants to do exactly the opposite to what the parents say. If

they say, "don't do," it wants to do exactly the thing they are saying not to do. And if they say "do," the child doesn't want to. Our mind too behaves exactly in this manner in ethical disciplines. Therefore, when one says, "be non-violent," the mind wants to be violent. If one says, "Be clean." then the mind says, "Let me not heed."

These laws and codes came into existence once we began behaving viciously. The culprit was born before the law. The rules and regulations came into existence as indiscipline was born. The mind wants to have *bhoga,* therefore, yoga came into existence. We all want the worldly enjoyments and not spiritual emancipation. Worldly experiences are natural but spiritual experiences are rare. They have to be known, earned and savoured. Our *citta* gravitates towards the pleasures of worldly experience. It easily gravitates towards violence and untruthfulness. This is called *pakṣabhāvanam* – going with the current. As violence is a natural instinct in man, it need not be taught. One need not be taught to lie. To hoard and to steal is but natural. The mind flows with the worldly current. The river of *citta* flows in that direction. As one builds a *bund* or dam to reverse the flow, the principles of *yama* and *niyama* are like a *bund* to check the mental current. So, whenever the river of *citta* flows against the good, we have to check its flow with contrary thoughts. That is called *pratipakṣa bhāvanam. Vitarka bādhana* has to be controlled with *pratipakṣa bhāvanam.* If the mind is demanding that we do violence, *pratipakṣa bhāvanam* doesn't say, "Be non-violent". *Pratipakṣa bhāvana* is a rational deliberation against dubious deliberation. If *vitarka bādhana* is a disease, *pratipakṣa bhāvanam* is its remedy. It is a process of analysing the thoughts and listening to the mind which wants to narrate its own version. Again on the same thought, the ego may throw a different version and the intellect as well as the consciousness may give their version. This is how we end up in indecisiveness. Sometimes the mind disagrees with the intelligence, or the intelligence disagrees with the ego and sometimes the consciousness disagrees with the intelligence. All these disagreements lead towards friction as nobody wants to listen to the conscience or the inner voice. Patañjali asks us to face friction and all diverting views in order to develop a balanced *citta*. An acrobat balances on a thin but strong rope. Similarly, a *sādhaka* has to balance on the rope of *pratipakṣa bhāvanam*, which is thin and subtle as well as strong and firm. It is for this reason that I say that the *dharma* of *yama* and *niyama* is very subtle and requires tremendous inner discipline to follow.

However, the principles of *yama* and *niyama* are difficult to follow as *citta* opposes them from within. Whenever we try to convince our own *citta*, it doubts and questions. Therefore, the *citta* has to be convinced through investigation and analysis. This investigation and analysis are in *yama* and *niyama* which act like *pratipakṣa bhāvanam*.

Think carefully about what I am saying. Whenever we go against the principles of *yama* and *niyama*, or whenever we go with the undisciplined mental current, there is *vitarka bādhana*. By observing *yama* and *niyama* our attitudes, our behaviour, our character, our thoughts and our actions co-operate to march ahead in the spiritual pursuit. They help us to conquer *prakṛti,* so that nature becomes our friend.

This reminds me of the epic *Mahābhārata.* I am tempted to tell you. In the story of the *Mahābhārata,* we read about the five Pāṇḍava brothers, Yudhiṣṭhira, Bhīma, Arjuna, Nakula and Sahadeva. Though these brothers were rightful rulers, injustice was done to them and they literally had to hide themselves.

The King Drupada had a daughter called Draupadi. When the king wanted her to get married, he arranged a bet. He tied a fish to the ceiling and a spoked wheel below, which rotated like a fan. A tank full of water was right below and the reflection of the fish on the water could be seen clearly. As the wheel was rotating, the fish too was circularly rotating, but in the opposite direction.

Now, the bet was that by looking into the water one had to shoot an arrow at the ceiling so that the arrow went right into the eye of the fish. Obviously, the arrow had to find a path between the spokes to reach the eye of the fish. Many princes came to win the beautiful princess – Draupadi. But to win Draupadi was not that easy. Only Arjuna hit the mark and succeeded.

Similarly, we too have a great challenge in front of us. If we are to shoot the arrow and hit the soul, we have to cross the *vṛtti-s* – the mental modifications, the *kleśa-s* – the afflictions, the *antarāya-s* – the obstacles, the *duḥkha-s* – the pains and *vitarka bādhana* – the dubious thoughts. It is as difficult as the bet to win Draupadi.

But we have to face all these impediments and come out of them. Patañjali wants us to be aware of all these problems and difficulties. If I say that the mountain is steep, it does not mean that you should not climb. It means, 'be careful'. If I say that there is a ditch, it does not mean, 'don't walk', but it means to take each step carefully. If I say, "don't dash against the wall", it means keep your eyes open so that you see the wall. The eyes of conscience have to be kept open, so that you cross the obstacles and solve the problems easily.

Having said about God, man, nature, the functions of mind and the ways to develop a stable mind, now let us move towards *aṣṭāṅga yoga* and see how we can apply the principles of yoga in our day to day practice of yoga *sādhanā*.

Chapter 2:

Application of Principles

AṢṬĀṄGA YOGA

Aṣṭāṅga yoga is the greatest and the noblest gift that was offered to man by the creator which Patañjali simplified for man to understand the subject in clear terms. It is the foundation and the pinnacle for most men in their yogic journey. Its beauty is that it can be adopted, adapted and absorbed according to one's physical, emotional and intellectual capacities. It can be practised in a mild form or in moderate or intensive forms. It yields fruit according to the quality of one's practice. When it is practised in a mild or gross form, its effect too will be mild. As the practice increases and becomes subtler and deeper, it reveals the esoteric phase of *aṣṭāṅga yoga* with its depth of meaning and its extensive effects.

Aṣṭāṅga yoga makes us aware of the various problems of man from ailments, sorrows and pains and at the same time, gives us hope that these pains and distresses can be avoided and eradicated through its practice. Patañjali says that we should build in us that defensive strength which helps in avoiding the pains that may arise in the future. The pains we are experiencing cannot be avoided, but can be reduced and unknown pains can be prevented by adhering to yogic practice and discipline.

Heyam duḥkham anāgatam II *(Y.S.,* II.16).

He guides us to live in the present, so that the future can take care of itself. He wants us to study the cause of distress and work on it for the eradication of pains and sorrows, so that we can become the masters of ourselves.

Here one should not mistake that yoga is done for the eradication of diseases. Patañjali wants everyone to work not only to prevent sorrows, pains and diseases, but to build up their physical, moral, mental and intellectual character in the ways of thinking and actions so that one's actions and discriminative thinkings are free from afflictions. He sums up the effect of yoga in Kaivalya Pāda and says,

Tataḥ kleśa karma nivṛttiḥ II *(Y.S.,* IV.30).

Then comes the end of afflictions and the beginning of *akliṣṭa vṛtti-s* – non-painful *vṛtti-s.*

Patañjali explains *aṣṭāṅga yoga* in detail in the *Sādhana Pāda,* the second chapter, though the thread of its *sādhana* is covered in all chapters. As the pains, problems, impediments and defects differ from person to person, Patañjali explains that in each *sādhaka,* at each stage, as he or she progresses, the depth of *aṣṭāṅga* – the eight aspects of yoga keep on changing and transforming.

For example, the *Samādhi Pāda* speaks mostly of *antaraṅga sādhanā* or the inner quest for those who are evolved in their spiritual quest. He explains in the *Sādhana Pāda* from the scratch for the uninitiated the *bahiraṅga sādhanā* or the external quest. Patañjali while explaining the effect of *āsana* says, *"tataḥ dvandvāḥ anabhighātaḥ II"* (*Y.S.,* II.48) which means that the differentiation between the muscles, limbs, joints, organs, mind, intelligence and self has to disappear to reach the state of equanimity.

To reach the state of equanimity, one finds the answer in *Samādhi Pāda* or chapter I. He says, *"tatpratiṣedhārtham ekatattva abhyāsaḥ II"*(*Y.S.,* I.32). It means that all the disparities and dualities which are mentioned above, have to be prevented and eradicated with a single minded effort or *sādhanā.* The moment the disparities strike the *sādhaka* in *sādhanā* or practice, his attention moves inwards. The moment the attention moves inwards, his *sādhanā* transforms into *antaraṅga sādhanā* or inner quest.

From here on the *sādhaka-s* whether external or internal move automatically towards *antarātma sādhanā* or innermost quest. In the *Vibhūti* and the *Kaivalya Pāda* (Chapter III and IV) Patañjali takes the aspirants directly to experience the seer or the soul or the *puruṣa* or the *ātman.*

SĀDHANĀ

What is *sādhanā?*

Sādhanā means practice. It also means dynamic effort. *Sādhanā* is a way of utilising our vehicles; the body, organs of action, senses of perception, mind, intellect and consciousness, to travel deeper towards the Self. The *sādhanā* begins when you apply your mind to think about the spiritual facts of life. *Sādhanā* has to be not only one-pointed effort but a multi-faceted effort to be attempted by the *sādhaka* from all sides in all the five sheaths of the body, namely *annamaya* – structural sheath of the body, *prāṇamaya* – vital layer of the body, *manomaya* or mind, *vijñānamaya* or intellectual body and spiritual body. The effort is both centripetal and centrifugal, but the direction of attention must be on the Self.

Children can never play with only one toy. They require a variety of toys. They want cars, jeeps, engines, trains as they are inquisitive to know about everything. They get bored quickly with one type or one thing. Even teenagers do not like having only one type of a game. In fact, we all love variety. *Sādhanā* provides us with a variety for practice. In spiritual *sādhanā* we behave like children and hence, Patañjali gives many methods to keep the mind of the *sādhaka* on the yogic path.

We know that the body is nourished and nurtured by food. We require vegetables, rice, wheat, milk and so on. We like having different tastes, different flavours. In fact, the health of the body requires calcium, magnesium, zinc, iron, vitamins, minerals and so on and so forth. Similarly, the *sādhaka* requires an all-round practice for spiritual growth and spiritual health. *Sādhanā* has to be used as a spiritual food. The *sādhaka* has to get spiritually nourished and nurtured. Therefore, his *sādhanā* has to have its vitamins, minerals and other nourishing factors. The food should be such that we are able to digest it easily and it should provide vital energy. Similarly, the *sādhanā* should be such that it ignites interest and adds to knowledge. It should be intellectually digestible, adoptable and acceptable according to the capacity of the *sādhaka*.

The *sādhanā* is ranked and categorised according to the progress of the *sādhaka*. As the depth of understanding increases the depth of *sādhanā* also increases.

In fact, the *sādhanā* is done to quench the thirst for knowledge of the Self. It is a search as well as a quest. As the search becomes exact, accurate and deep; the phase and depth of *sādhanā* changes.

Sādhanā is wrapped up in three layers; outer, inner and innermost, which are called *bahiraṅga sādhanā, antaraṅga sādhanā* and *antarātma sādhanā* respectively. Traditionally, in *aṣṭāṅga yoga*, the first five aspects, namely, *yama, niyama, āsana, prāṇāyāma* and *pratyāhāra* are considered as *bahiraṅga sādhanā, dhāraṇā* and *dhyāna* as *antaraṅga sādhanā*. In *samādhi* the *antarātma sādhanā* is hidden and undisclosed. However, through the experience of *sabīja* and *nirbīja samādhi* one reaches the state of *kevalāvasthā* or a state of aloneness with fullness in body, mind and soul. This is the end part of *antarātma sādhanā as one's sādhanā* begins from a seeker and ends in reaching the state of a seer or the soul.

Patañjali begins the subject with the definition of yoga as restraining the consciousness from the rays of thought waves.

Yogaḥ cittavṛtti nirodhaḥ // (*Y.S.*, I.2).

This very *sūtra* is enough to convey that Patañjali started yoga with *antaraṅga sādhanā*. As we are made up of gross *indriya-s* like body, organs of action, senses of perception, mind and subtle *indriya-s* like the intelligence, ego, consciousness and conscience; probably the intelligence of man in those days must have been very high for Patañjali to start yoga with *antaraṅga sādhanā* with the subtlest of senses. If one refers to the text from *sūtra-s* 33 to 39 of the *Samādhi Pāda*, Patañjali implicitly explains *aṣṭāṅga yoga* in such a subtle form as if it is *antaraṅga sādhanā*.

After finishing the first chapter, Patañjali must have realised that his work may not be understood by an average intellectual, so he attends to their needs in *Sādhanā Pāda*, so that they too can reach the goal of yoga making them channel their senses of perception first inwards or towards the in-depth of the body and shows the ways of acquiring control of themselves to move in the quest of the soul. As he begins from the senses of perception and organs of action, it is called *bahiraṅga sādhanā*.

Antaraṅga sādhaka-s are asked to practise yoga in order to restrain the movements or fluctuations of consciousness. However, the average intellectual is caught in *duḥkha* – sorrow, distress, disease and pain. Therefore Patañjali explains *bahiraṅga sādhanā* for them to understand yoga as *duḥkha-vṛtti nirodha.* That is how yoga was recognised as an alternative complimentary treatment of diseases. He wants the common man to get rid of *duḥkha-vṛtti-s* first before he moves towards *citta-vṛtti nirodha.*

Patañjali wants the yoga *sādhaka* to get rid of small hiccups that put a block on the quest for the spiritual kingdom. Hence, Patañjali guides the *sādhaka-s* to prevent or cure those troubling diseases, sorrows and despairs, which are the hiccups of the life force of men, so that one day they may taste the unalloyed and untainted bliss forcing themselves from all these impediments and obstacles to experience what emancipation is like.

In one *sūtra,* Patañjali defines the effect of yoga and induces all to take to yoga.

Yogāṅgānuṣṭhānāt aśuddhikṣaye jñānadīptiḥ āvivekakhyāteḥ *//* (*Y.S.,* II.28)

Here, Patañjali sums up the effects of the eight-fold yogic practice saying that yoga not only destroys the impurities of body, mind and consciousness at the physical, moral, mental, intellectual and spiritual levels, but it generates knowledge and kindles the light until the crown of wisdom shines and radiates in glory.

Watch the sequence of the effects explained by Patañjali. First is *aśuddhikṣaya* and then *jñānadīptīḥ. Aśuddhikṣaya* means eradication of impurities and *jñānadīptīḥ* means kindling the light of intelligence for higher knowledge. When darkness is removed, light follows. Hence, he says, remove the impurities for purity to dawn. Make the knowledge to shine so that ignorance is removed.

THE *YOGĀṄGA-S*

Yama niyama āsana prāṇāyāma pratyāhāra
dhāraṇā dhyāna samādhayaḥ aṣṭau aṅgāni // (*Y.S.*, II.29)

Yogāṅga-s are eight in number. These are *yama, niyama, asana, prāṇāyāma, pratyāhāra, dhāraṇā, dhyāna* and *samādhi.* Each of these yogic aspects brings *vṛtti nirodha* in different forms at different levels.

Table 9. - *Aṣṭāṅga Yoga* and *Vṛtti Nirodha*

Yama	——	*guṇa-vṛtti nirodha*
Niyama	——	*svabhāva-vṛtti nirodha*
Āsana	——	*snāyu-vṛtti nirodha*
Prāṇāyāma	——	*prāṇa-vṛtti nirodha*
Pratyāhāra	——	*mano-vṛtti nirodha*
Dhāraṇā	——	*buddhi-vṛtti nirodha*
Dhyāna	——	*ahaṁkāra-vṛtti nirodha*
Samādhi	——	*antaḥkaraṇa-vṛtti nirodha*

Yama means moral and ethical injunctions. *Niyama* means fixed and established observances to be followed. *Āsana* means posture. *Prāṇāyāma* means regulating and restraining the breath in order to channel the energy. *Pratyāhāra* means withdrawing the senses from the external objects and then to internalise them towards their source. *Dhāraṇā* means concentration or attention. *Dhyāna* means contemplation or meditation. *Samādhi* means total absorption. *Aṣṭa* means eight. *Aṅga* means limbs or constituent parts. Thus *aṣṭāṅga yoga* comprises of the above eight aspects or eight constituents.

Table 10. - The Three Tiers of *Sādhanā*

SĀDHANĀ

BAHIRAṄGA	***ANTARAṄGA***	***ANTARĀTMA***
yama	*dhāraṇā*	*samādhi*
niyama	*dhyāna*	
āsana		
prāṇāyāma		
pratyāhāra		

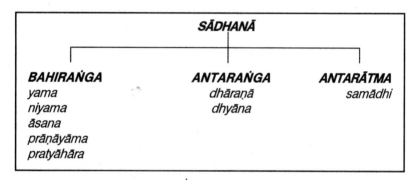

These eight aspects of yoga are divided into three tiers or compartments for the sake of convenience or according to the capability of intelligence of man of today. As man is instinctively weak in moral approach, *yama* and *niyama* are given as the first and foremost steps in *aṣṭāṅga yoga*. Man by nature is susceptible to violence in words, thoughts, and deeds, lies, covetousness, libertinism and greed. Patañjali wants the *sādhaka-s* organs of action clear though tempted by the senses of perception and mind. So for the *sādhaka* first discipline is to keep the organs of action clean. See – *ahiṁsā satya asteya brahmacarya aparigrahāḥ yamāḥ II* (*Y.S.,* II.30).

Niyama is meant to keep clean the senses of perception by cleanliness, contentment, religious fervour, understanding the views on the Self and surrender of oneself to God. *"śauca santoṣa tapaḥ svādhyāya Īśvarapraṇidhānāni niyamāḥ II"* (*Y.S.,* II.32).

If *yama* is meant for keeping the organs of action or *karmendriya-s* clean, *niyama* is to keep the senses of perception-*jñānendriya-s* clean. As such *yama* and *niyama* are *bahiraṅga sādhanā.* These ethical principles are applicable to one and all. *Āsana, prāṇāyāma* and *pratyāhāra* are *antaraṅga sādhanā* since we enter into the yogic world through these gates. And *dhāraṇā, dhyāna* and *samādhi* are *antarātma sādhanā.* Here we enter into the regime of the Self. One has to unfold these three wrappers or coverings through these eight aspects of yoga. At the same time, each wrapper or covering contains the gross, subtle and subtlest aspects, which one should keep in mind.

Table 11. - Simplified Categorisation

SĀDHANĀ

BAHIRAṄGA	***ANTARAṄGA***	***ANTARĀTMA***
yama	*āsana*	*dhāraṇā*
niyama	*prāṇāyāma*	*dhyāna*
	pratyāhāra	*samādhi*

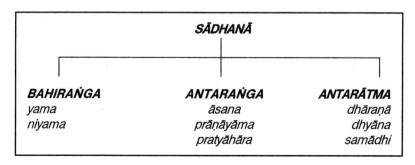

The *sādhaka-s* of yore had very strong willpower. Their incredible devotion compared to today's ways is inexpressible. We might be showing progress in worldly achievements but we are nowhere as far as spiritual achievements are concerned. Therefore, *aṣṭāṅga yoga* was treated as a single unit then. Today, the intellectual level of man is average in spiritual kingdom. It is described compartmentally as *bahiraṅga, antaraṅga* and *antarātma sādhanā* to grasp the subject of yoga with ease.

THE MAP OF THE HUMAN BEING

The aim of yoga is to conquer *prakṛti* and reach the seer to experience what true realisation is. *Prakṛti* is the primordial matter and *puruṣa* is the sentient being. They are conjunct. We human beings are the result of this conjunction. We have *citta* – the consciousness, with *buddhi* – Intelligence, *ahaṁkāra* – ego or 'I' consciousness and *manas* – mind. Since the *guṇa-s* or qualities rule over the *manas, buddhi* and *ahaṁkāra,* each one of them can be coined as *sāttvika buddhi* – illumined intelligence, *rājasika buddhi* – active and fluctuating intelligence and *tāmasika buddhi* – stagnated and inert intelligence. The same can be applied to the ego as well as to the mind.

Now, let us consider the body. The body has five elements. Each element has its gross existence with its subtle qualities. The five gross elements of the body are earth, water, fire, air and ether. The subtle or infra-atomic structures of the five elements are smell,

Table 12: Map of the Human Being

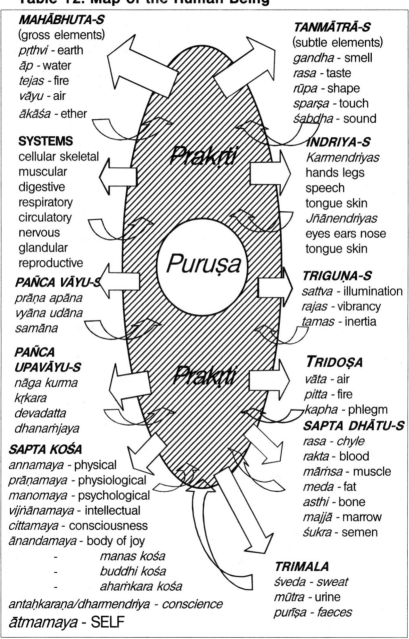

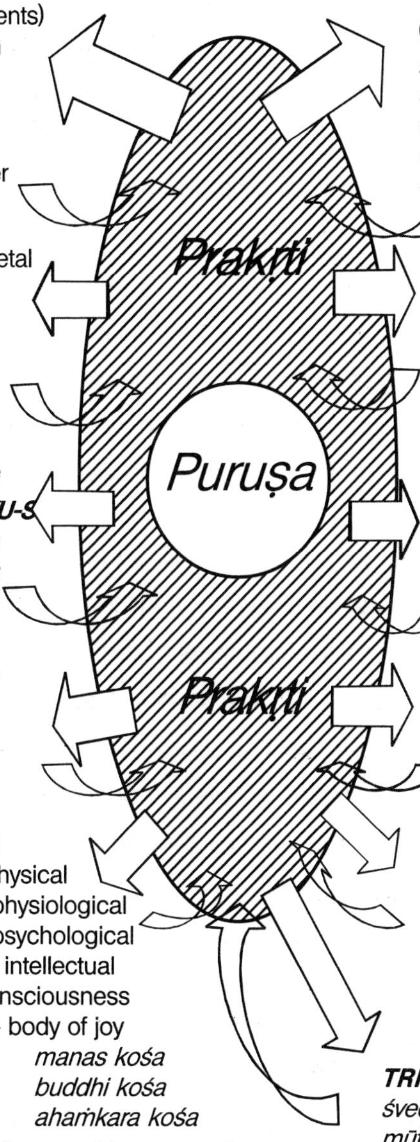

MAHĀBHUTA-S
(gross elements)
pṛthvi - earth
āp - water
tejas - fire
vāyu - air
ākāśa - ether

SYSTEMS
cellular skeletal
muscular
digestive
respiratory
circulatory
nervous
glandular
reproductive

PAÑCA VĀYU-S
prāṇa apāna
vyāna udāna
samāna

PAÑCA UPAVĀYU-S
nāga kurma
kṛkara
devadatta
dhanaṁjaya

SAPTA KOŚA
annamaya - physical
prāṇamaya - physiological
manomaya - psychological
vijñānamaya - intellectual
cittamaya - consciousness
ānandamaya - body of joy
- *manas kośa*
- *buddhi kośa*
- *ahaṁkara kośa*

antaḥkaraṇa/dharmendriya - conscience
ātmamaya - SELF

TANMĀTRĀ-S
(subtle elements)
gandha - smell
rasa - taste
rūpa - shape
sparṣa - touch
śabdha - sound

INDRIYA-S
Karmendriyas
hands legs
speech
tongue skin
Jñānendriyas
eyes ears nose
tongue skin

TRIGUṆA-S
sattva - illumination
rajas - vibrancy
tamas - inertia

TRIDOṢA
vāta - air
pitta - fire
kapha - phlegm

SAPTA DHĀTU-S
rasa - chyle
rakta - blood
māṁsa - muscle
meda - fat
asthi - bone
majjā - marrow
śukra - semen

TRIMALA
śveda - sweat
mūtra - urine
purīṣa - faeces

taste, shape, touch and sound. Out of these five elements of our body, the three elements and their qualities act as a playground for life to function. These are *āp, tej* and *vāyu.* These three elements and their energies create *tridoṣa, sapta dhātu-s* and *trimala.* The three humours of the body are called *tridoṣa* which are *vāta* – wind, *pitta* – bile and *kapha* or *śleṣma* – phlegm. The *sapta dhātu* or the seven ingredients are, *rasa* – chyle, *rakta* – blood, *māṁsa* – muscles, *meda* – fat, *asthi* – bones, *majjā* – bone marrow and *śukra* – semen. The wastage of the body called *trimala* are *sveda* – sweat, *purīṣa* – faeces, *mūtra* – urine. The three humours of the body along with the seven ingredients play a major role in the function and balance of the metabolic process.

The energy in the form of *pañca-vāyu-s* and *pañca-upavāyu-s*, activates and metabolise the various systems of the body and generate new energy. All the functions of the body depend upon these *vāyu-s.* These are *prāṇa, apāna, vyāna, udāna* and *samāna.* Each has its own function and location of work allotted in the body and our consciousness is able to control them by will and energy. Each *vāyu* has its assistant – an *upavāyu.* These assisting *vāyu-s* aid the principle *vāyu-s.* These *upavāyu-s* are *nāga, kūrma, kṛkara, devadatta* and *dhanaṁjaya.*

Apart from all these, we have the cellular, skeletal, muscular, digestive, circulatory, respiratory, nervous, excretory, reproductive and glandular systems. These physico-physiological and neuro-spiritual functions and their effects leave their impressions upon the mind and its activities to a great extent.

The five senses of perception, eyes, ears, nose, tongue and skin yield the sensations of seeing, hearing, smelling, tasting and touching. The five organs of action, hands, legs, mouth, genitals and excretory organs help us with functions such as holding, walking, talking, reproducing and excreting.

Again, if we give a little thought, then we find that we are made up of *saptakośa-s* – seven sheaths. They are the *annamaya kośa* – physical body, *prāṇamaya kośa* – physiological body, *manomaya kośa* – psychological body, *vijñānamaya kośa* – intellectual body, *cittamaya kośa* – the body of consciousness, *ānandamaya kośa* – the body of joy, *antaḥkaraṇa kośa* – body of conscience – *dharmendriya* links one to *ātmamaya kośa* – the body of the Self. Thus, we are made up of body, mind and soul. Look into the geography of the body and the mind and how these components are expanded. We need to train and energise them and lead these forces towards the soul. For this we need discipline to take all these vehicles on the healthy path through *aṣṭāṅga yoga* to rest in the abode of the soul. So let us see the geography and the terrain of *aṣṭāṅga yoga* as we travel with its *sādhanā*.

When you see any country on the globe, the country looks small compared to the globe. Again, a globe or our own planet Earth is a small atom compared to the vast number of planets in the universe. Similarly, when you look at *aṣṭāṅga yoga* it seems as though it is a small part of the *Yoga Sūtra-s* of Patañjali but it covers the microcosm of man and the macrocosm of the Universe.

As a map shows the geographical situation of an area, I give you a map of *aṣṭāṅga yoga* so that you know how big it is. Through this map you know its situation, its dimension and its expansion. Each aspect is spread and amplified and at certain places it also shows the subtleness and sharpness (see table 12).

KRIYĀ YOGA

The eight aspects of yoga form a triangular frame in the form of *kriyā yoga*, namely, *tapas* – passionate zeal, *svādhyāya* – self-study and *Īśvara praṇidhāna* – surrender to God. These three aspects *tapas, svādhyāya* and *Īśvara praṇidhāna* are like the three sides forming the triangle of *aṣṭāṅga yoga*.

Yama, niyama, āsana and *prāṇāyāma* are the base of the triangle as *tapas*. *Pratyāhāra, dhāraṇā* and *dhyāna* are one side of the triangle as *svādhyāya*. *Samādhi* as the other side of the triangle as *Īśvara praṇidhāna*. (see table 13).

TAPAS

Tapas is a way of discipline to free oneself from *tāpa-s* or afflictions. *Tapas* is to keep the body, senses and mind free from impurities and cultivate cleanliness. Nobody can practise unless there is a burning zeal within. This zeal should be expressive as well as impressive. It is very easy to claim that you are very much interested and keen in yoga. Often people come and say that they are ready to give their life for yoga. To say that your life is meant for yoga is easy. But when you find that yoga is hard to do and difficult to follow you give up. It is not difficult to begin yoga but to continue and maintain the practice irrespective of gain or loss, success or failure, achievement or non-achievement is very difficult. Because of this it is called *tapas.*

When *Ṛsi* Chyavana sat for *tapas,* a mound of ants formed covering him. For years he remained surrounded by those mounds. By chance, Princess Sukanyā who came to see the forest noticed the shining eyes behind the mound and being innocent pricked the two shining eyes which started bleeding, making Chyavana blind. But, despite this he still continued his *tapas.*

When Viśvāmitra *ṛṣi* was doing *tapas.* Menakā the damsel from heaven came to disturb him. His *tapas* was disturbed by her and he fell in love with her. They had a daughter called Śakuntalā. When Viśvāmitra realised his downfall, he had to restart his *tapas.*

Disturbances may come or you may fall into the trap of temptations. On account of these, you may be criticised, you may be hated, you may be disrespected and humiliated. The *vāsanā-s* – desires may haunt you. Still, you have to continue your practice as *tapas* with zeal. It requires a burning desire and will to continue. That is why one needs willpower to practise under all circumstances or situations. In turn *tapas* re-charges the willpower. If will is like a fuel, *tapas* is like a flame of the fire.

SVĀDHYĀYA

Then comes *svādhyāya*. *Sva* means one's own. *Adhyāya* means study. It also means a lesson. *Svādhyāya* is to study and to 'know thy self'. It also means 'to study on one's own'. It is to understand 'Who I am' and 'What I am.' through the study of the scriptures and the repetition of *mantra-s* or *vaidika* recitation. *Svādhyāya* is supported indirectly by *tapas*. *Svādhyāya* without *tapas* will be just gathering knowledge.

Svādhyāya helps one to scrutinise one's *tapas*. As a matter of fact, it guides and strengthens the *tapas* to go in the right direction making it meaningful by cultivating tolerance and patience in the practitioner. Without the knowledge of *svādhyāya*, or study of the Self, *tapas* becomes a meaningless and aimless pursuit.

If *tapas* guides one to do right *karma* – work, *svādhyāya* brings right *jñāna* – knowledge. Study and understand the basic principle behind each *karma* so that the *karma* becomes worthy. *Karma* and *jñāna* together inspire a devotional attitude in the practitioner. This is *bhakti* or *Īśvara praṇidhāna*.

ĪŚVARA PRAṆIDHĀNA

Īśvara praṇidhāna is a complete surrender of oneself to God. For this we need to develop an inner state to gravitate towards the Supreme.

Before doing any kind of ritual or religious rite, we say that we are doing it to please the Supreme. At the end also, we say that we are sacrificing the fruits of the rituals to God. At the start, we say, *"Bhagavad prītyartham"*. It means to please the God. At the end we say, *"Sri Krishnārpaṇamastu"*. It means every action and its fruits, everything is surrendered to Lord Krishna. Though it is an Indian custom, it has a great meaning of conveying the presence of the Universal Force as well as showing the way of non-attachment. As man's nature is selfish, these words *'Bhagavad prītyartham'*, and *'Sri Krishnārpaṇamastu'*, guide man to change the selfish attitude into selfless attitude so that every act of his changes for the good of mankind. The Supreme is prayed to and praised so that He blesses and showers peace and bliss on all beings.

WHAT IS *AṢṬĀṄGA YOGA*?

Having explained what *kriyā yoga* stands for, now let me go into *aṣṭāṅga yoga* with its eight petals, namely, *yama, niyama, āsana, prāṇāyāma, pratyāhāra, dhāraṇā, dhyāna,* and *sāmadhi.*

Yama, niyama, āsana, prāṇāyāma and *pratyāhāra* is *tapas. Dhāraṇā* and *dhyāna* is *svādhyāya. Samādhi* is *Īśvara praṇidhāna.* The first seven aspects of *aṣṭāṅga yoga* are *abhyāsa sādhanā* whereas, *samādhi* is *paramavairāgya sādhanā.* Both *abhyāsa* and *vairāgya* go together while doing *sādhanā* and when the *abhyāsa* becomes intense, *vairāgya* too becomes intense and finally leads towards *paramavairāgya* – supreme detachment.

Aṣṭāṅga yoga means the eight aspects or eight petals of yoga. They are very significant in making man a complete being. It is a perfect spiritual path. It is well thought of from all angles of man's growth by Patañjali. A man becomes complete when his physical body, moral behaviour, mental activities, intellectual discrimination and spiritual benevolence are fully developed.

Table 13. - The Triangle of Kriyã Yoga

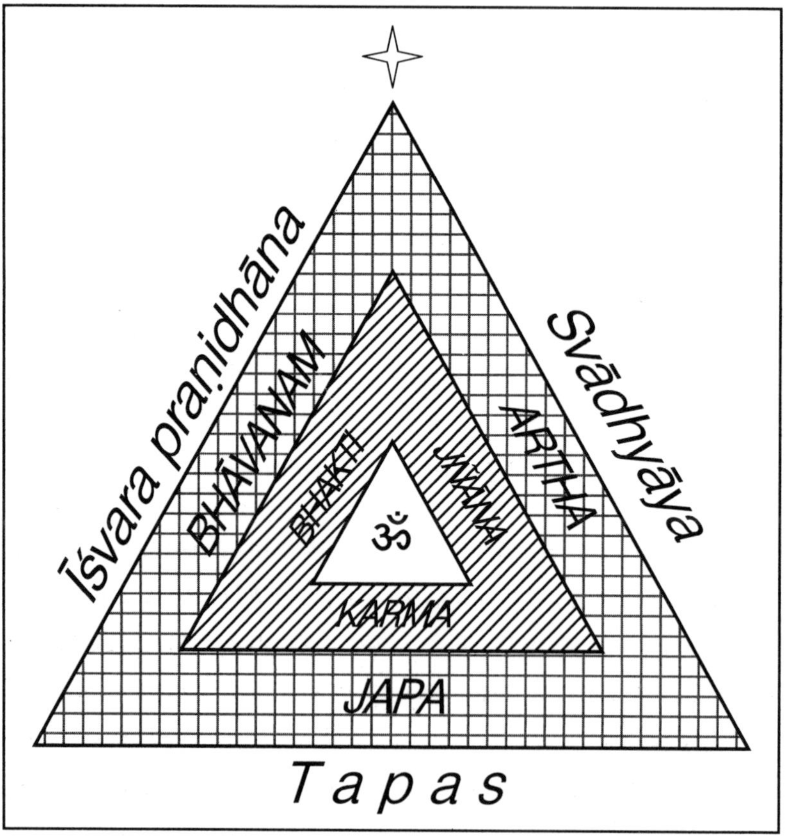

Yama and *niyama* mould man morally with ethical practice. *Āsana* and *prāṇāyāma* trim the body and mind by providing physical, physiological, psychological and mental health. *Pratyāhāra* controls man's mental activities, reminding him that he is not an animal but a human being who can control himself. *Pratyāhāra* is a check on the mind in order to keep the senses of perception and organs of action free from extravagant sensual enjoyments. It disciplines the outgoing flow of the senses so that the practitioner maintains the energy to remain passive in its place. Therefore, *pratyāhāra* is a kind of 'tableland'. It consolidates and stabilises the qualities and progress that has been learnt from *yama* to *prāṇāyāma*. *Dhāraṇā* guides the *citta* of man so that his disarrayed attention is focused on one point or place. *Dhyāna* saturates the attention to go deeper towards the source of existence so that the intellectual and conscious energy melts in the seat of the soul. When consciousness and intelligence melts, it is *samādhi*. *Samādhi* is a state in which one loses the sense of one's own existence. Nothing else remains except the core – the *puruṣa*.

The first two aspects of yoga, namely, *yama* and *niyama* are the gatekeepers of our spiritual domain. There can be no spiritual empire without *yama* and *niyama*. Even a spiritual master has to be measured with the scales of *yama* and *niyama* before one can accept him as his master. Without *yama* and *niyama* it is not possible to reach the spiritual heights.

Yama and *niyama* change the *guṇa-doṣa* into *guṇa-śuddhi* or purity. In one way it can be termed as defects of the *guṇa-vṛtti nirodha*. *Guṇa* means characteristic in each individual. Our character depends upon the lamination of wisdom, predominance of activation and inertic or lazy characteristics hidden within the natureas well as in man known as *sattva, rajas* and *tamas as these mould* and shape man according to these three *guṇa-s.* The *rajoguṇa* and *tamoguṇa* pollute the *citta* and the *citta* appears with its *durguṇa-s* – bad qualities or evil properties and propensities.

YAMA

Though in the previous section I spoke in brief about *yama* and *niyama,* here a detailed picture of *yama* and *niyama* is given. The principles of *yama* are *ahiṁsā* – non-violence, *satya* – truthfulness, *asteya* – non-greediness, *brahmacarya* – chastity or continence, *aparigraha* – non-possession or desirelessness.

Man has been caught from time immemorial in the web of perverse thoughts, emotions and actions. He becomes complicated and susceptible to *hiṁsā, asatya, steya, abrahmacarya, parigraha, aśauca, asantoṣa, atapas, asvādhyāya* and on account of these weakneses devilry appears taking the place of divinity.

Yama explains the rules and regulations that are to be observed and followed in life to change his defective thoughts and actions towards constructive thoughts. This instinctive intellectual weakness of man is described as want of moral conduct in man to change his way of thinking and living to lead a righteous and virtuous life. These are meant to bring purity and at the same time it enables man to live a calm and cool life not only within himself, but also to make use of it in society. The principles of *yama* remind us that we are not only individual beings but also social beings. Its code of conduct helps one to know how to behave with oneself and with others. As we expect others to behave with us, we need to check whether we behave with others in the same manner. This is learnt by the principles of *yama* through building the right mannerisms in the forms of *yama* and *niyama* to reach the Ultimate aim in life – the sight of the Soul.

Before thinking of the ultimate goal in yoga, one has to know the cause for violence to justify the act of violence. The cause behind a violent act might be hidden within oneself though dumped on an outsider. It might be caused by greed, anger or delusion. The violence could be mild, medium or intense in degree. It may be done directly or indirectly. Someone may induce or seduce one into violence at any time, place or circumstance irrespective of caste, class, creed, religion or sex.

Patañjali explains this in clear terms in *"vitarkaḥ hiṁsādayaḥ kṛta kārita anumoditāḥ lobha krodha moha pūrvakaḥ mṛdu madhya adhimātraḥ duḥkha ajñāna anantaphalāḥ iti pratipakṣabhāvanam II"* (*Y.S.*,II.34). It means uncertain knowledge giving rise to violence, whether done directly or indirectly or condoned is caused by greed, anger or delusion in mind of moderate or intense degree. It results in endless pains and ignorance. Through introspection comes the end of pain and ignorance.

One has to analyse, investigate, enquire, introspect and weigh before committing violence. For instance, to follow *ahiṁsā* or non-violence, we may wonder what kind of intelligence is required. It may be that one's non-violence may prove to be violence to another. Therefore, one cannot just be non-violent as that will result in an impotency of vigour and valour. Non-violence may be a precise judgement in that spur of the moment. But it needs a careful intelligence like the scales of justice to balance violence and non-violence so that negative and destructive thoughts and actions are replaced by positive constructive thoughts and actions.

To taste the fruit one has to first peel the skin of the fruit. Similarly, to reach the depth or the pulp of each aspect of *yama* and *niyama,* one has to go on peeling layer after layer of the mixed feelings in ones action to understand and correct them in order to savour its nectar.

When we read yoga texts, we think that we can immediately adopt and adapt them as they are structurally explained. But, it is not so. It needs careful study and disciplined practice. For example, anger, cruelty, ferocity, harassment, teasing, ragging; all these come under violence. If we watch our intellectual and emotional weather carefully, we discover that violence is hidden or attenuated in us physically and mentally at all levels. Therefore, I said that we have to carefully weigh.

Now, take *satya,* when we are in the witness box, we say that we tell the truth and take an oath in the name of God, the *Bible,* the *Koran* or the *Bhagavad Gītā.* But when the time comes, we forget that oath and knowingly or consciously say an untruth to save ourselves.

We may not know the truth, but with our imagination we add to the heard statements and follow an untruth. If one consciously speaks untruthfully, it is definitely *asatya,* but speaking untruthfully or saying unconsciously by a slip of the tongue becomes the seed of *asatya.* Dishonesty, deceiving, befooling, cheating are all the facets of *asatya.*

Steya means to steal. We may not be thieves, we may not commit burglary. But we are covetous. This tendency leads towards *steya.* The greed could be for name, fame and money but greed is a never ending hunger. Greed is never fulfilled.

Today, people steal ideas. Therefore one has to get lawfully sanctioned copyrights and patents. Is it not stealing if someone presents another person's work as one's own? Is not stealing of another's intelligence, a deceit?

Often people try to imitate somebody's style of life and in doing so they go far from their own life style. Stealing the style of another, may cause a great change to ones personality, behaviour and attitude, but it causes one to go away from one's own truth.

Brahmacarya does not mean total continence. If so, our sages would not have introduced *gṛhasthāśrama* – the married life. It brings sanctity to the inner drive of sex in human beings, hence, *gṛhasthāśrama* was introduced. Today, freedom to act as one likes has resulted in the net of the king of demons – AIDS.

According to my understanding *brahmacarya* means controlled celibacy. That is why married life is suggested by the scriptures to bring contentment with a disciplined sex life, conducive to *brahmacarya* developing moral and mental strength from within.

Parigraha means possession. As long as there is attachment to life, there is *parigraha*. Greed is *parigraha*. One can say that one is non greedy and non-possessive but the hidden instinct to possess is there in all. Some may be able to give up material possessiveness but what about their knowledge? How many are willing to open the secret chamber of knowledge that they have? This intellectual possessiveness is so deep within us that it possesses us even after death. The very cause of possessiveness leads us towards further lives and further *karma-s*.

NIYAMA

Now let me divert your attention from *yama* to *niyama*. The five principles of *yama* – non-violence, truthfulness, non-stealing, celibacy and non-covetousness are not only inter-dependent but are inter-woven in the *niyama-s*. Let us know what the *niyama-s* are. The current of *yama* is to reflect and to workout in such a way that what should not be done should be avoided as far as possible, whereas in *niyama*, one has to practice and follow of what to do and what has to be done as a principle of life. In fact both *yama* and *niyama* are so much interrelated which helps us to a great extent in transforming our behaviour for a good use in life. Hence my advice would be to use the principles of *yama* and *niyama* to live an ethical life.

Niyama is a straightforward discipline *dinacaryā* – a daily routine for a *sādhaka*. It is a pilot scheme to lead a yogic life.

The principles of *niyama* are *śauca* – cleanliness, *santoṣa* – contentment, *tapas* – austerity, *svādhyāya* – self-study and *Īśvara praṇidhāna* – devotion towards the Supreme. We have to adopt these principles for the whole of our lives. By nature man is slow, easy-going, lazy and often lives an undisciplined life. *Niyama* brings the discipline and breaks the inertia by shaping the inner tendencies to follow the disciplined yogic path. If *yama* brings *guṇa-śuddhi* or merited qualities then *niyama* brings *svabhāva-śuddhi* or cleanliness in one's innate disposition.

Śaucha – cleanliness includes like brushing the teeth, having a bath and combing the hair are daily routines of external cleanliness which must not end at these levels. But one has to give thought to internal cleanliness also. We take a bath to clean the outer body, but how do we bathe each cell of the inner body? It is through good blood circulation and flow of energy in abundance. As we are drawn with physical, physiological and mental stress factors in our daily lives, we hinder the proper supply of blood and flow of energy and sap the body. This is the reason for an increase in the number of heart problems. Arteries get blocked and angioplasty–by-pass surgery–has become the order of the day. These things happen on account of non-attention to the cleansing of the internal body. Many diseases like constipation, diabetes, liver problems, urinary disorders and other diseases build up disturbing a clean healthy living.

Wrong food, wrong habits, wrong exertion, wrong way of living, late food, late nights, indiscipline are all *aśauca karma-s.*

Let me draw your attention to Patañjali and see what he says on the effect of *śauca.* He says, *śaucāt svāṅgajugupsā paraiḥ asaṁsargaḥ II,* and *sattvaśuddhi saumanasya aikāgrya indriyajaya ātmadarśana yogyatvāni ca II,* it means that the cleanliness of body develops disinterest to touch others' bodies and self-gratification fades. Therefore, one develops abhorrence, a kind of disinterest for one's own body. This aversion towards one's own body leads towards detachment and the mind builds up purity, calmness and cheerfulness. The mind becomes fit and ripe for the intelligence to develop the power of concentration and attention to go inwards to discover the core of the being.

Contentment undoubtedly does not come with ease. Yet it brings with it satisfaction and checks the craving for food; helps in curbing desire, anger, ambition, greed and develops *saumanasya* – benevolence.

Tapas

Tapas is self-discipline. The body is a treacherous friend. The senses of perception cheat us. We don't know at what time the body and the senses will allure us. We need to burn these desires by passionate, yogic practice. Just as passion forces the lover to meet with the beloved, the passion for practice must be such that we meet our beloved, the Self within.

This burning desire, this passion leads us towards *svādhyāya* and *Īśvara praṇidhāna.* The study and practice of yoga with devotional attention on God is *tapas.*

If *aparigraha* is the subtlest principle among *yama-s. Īśvara praṇidhāna* is the subtlest in the *niyama-s.* Similarly, *abhiniveśa* is the subtlest of all the *kleśa-s. Abhiniveśa* is love for life, an attachment and pride in ones existence, as well as fear of death. Self-preservation is inborn. To conquer the temporal desires, we need to understand properly the three properties of *niyama-s,* namely, *tapas, svādhyāya* and *Īśvara praṇidhāna.*

We know we are mortals. We know that this life ends at anytime, at any place. We also know that life is not permanent. Though the body perishes and we die, we know that there is a continuity of life even after death and life begins again with a new birth. Still, at the moment of death, fear does not leave even a wise man. This fear of death – *abhiniveśa* is hidden in *parigraha.* The love and attachment to what one has, whether it is material wealth, one's wife, husband or children does not diminish. But who knows, at the time of death the love and attachment to what we own may increase. The effect of *parigraha* leaves behind the imprints called *vāsanā* – desire – on the causal body so that they carry these imprints in a subtle form even after death. The strong will to live carries *abhiniveśa* into the new life with a new fresh body. This is possessiveness or attachment to carry on with the cycle of life and death.

Therefore, Patañjali says that the knowledge of past and future unfolds when one is free from greed for possessions – *parigraha.*

Aparigrahasthairye janmakathaṁtā saṁbodhaḥ II, it means that through *aparigraha,* the *sādhaka* gets the knowledge of his past and future lives. Each kind of attachment leads to a new life. When we fail to get something in this life, we often say "Oh! I will get it in the next life." This way we sow the seed of a new life. Though all of us think and talk highly about *mokṣa* or liberation, this may remain a dream thought only, as we may not be ready for that emancipated liberation.

The non-possessiveness reminds the *sādhaka* of how he gets entangled in the chain of lives because of possessiveness. That is how he gets a clear view of his life as an open book to read. He connects all his attachments, achievements, hopes, ambitions and desires, to his previous lives. He carefully dissects his own *citta* and totally restrains from accepting anything from anyone and works to reduce the storage of *karma*.

With *Īśvara praṇidhāna* as the needle and *vairāgya* as the thread, he conquers *abhiniveśa* and *aparigraha*. As the thread follows the needle, *vairāgya* follows *Īśvara praṇidhāna*.

A latent nature of assaulting, insulting, harming, dextrously speaking, material or intellectual stealing or forgery, love with lust, selfish motives and hoarding lead one towards attachment. They fertilise the land of *avidyā*, for the *kleśa-s* to grow and lead one to do untoward action as *kukarma*.

Earlier, I spoke about *sakāma karma* and *niṣkāma karma*. Action done with desire is *sakāma* and a desireless action is *niṣkāma*. Bad action is *duṣkarma*. Evil-minded action is *kukarma*. *Sakāma karma* also called *sukāma karma* done with good intention leads to a happy state of mind. *Duṣkarma* or *kukarma*, done with bad or evil intention, leads one towards spite and hatred. *Karma-s* done against the principles of *yama* and *niyama* throb and pulsate with the high fever of *vitarka bādhana* in the pit of sinful acts (see table - 14).

So *yama* and *niyama* teach us to listen to the inner voice of the conscience so that the *sādhaka* does not go in wrong directions. An ice bag is kept on the head and the body at the time of high fever. The body is sponged with cold water or eau de cologne. Similarly, one needs to cool the mind with *pratipakṣa bhāvanam.*

Yama and *niyama* are definitely difficult disciplines. Oaths and promises do not help as one may not keep the promises. Hence, try to live as far as possible with these principles so that the intelligence gets ripened and the conscience develops the sensitivity to stick to good *karma* otherwise you may lose the track. Adopt and absorb these two principles with prudence so that the mind develops on its own to tread the moral principles.

Therefore, watch the ten principles of *yama* and *niyama* without under or over emphasis. When you balance these, the difficulty in following them is lessened. Do not adopt one as an absolute entity but adopt all as far as possible equally. Do justice to all the principles of *yama* and *niyama* so that you are not biased or tilted or gravitate towards one side.

ĀSANA

The galaxy of thoughts that gathers in the mind does not allow the mind for a single-pointed attention. If you do something unusual, curiosity brings people to gather around you. Similarly when *citta* tries to do something unusual, galaxy of thoughts gathers around the *citta*.

Therefore, one has to reduce the galaxy of thoughts through *sādhanā*. It is with total attention and devotion in practice of *āsana*, *prāṇāyāma* or *dhyāna* that we learn to be courageous, free from

Table 14. - The Classification of Action
(The intention behind the action decides the nature of *karma*)

KARMA

SAKĀMA

Kṛta	***Kārita***	***Anumodita***
Sukarma	*Sukarma*	*Sukarma*
Kukarma	*Kukarma*	*Kukarma*
Duṣkarma	*Duṣkarma*	*Duṣkarma*

NIṢKĀMA

(kauśala karma) is possible only by *abhyāsa & vairāgya*

Patañjali, in his yoga *sūtras* refers to four types of *karma* which are similar to those explained above; he says,

i) *śukla karma*	white	*sakāma karma, sukarma*
ii) *kṛṣṇa karma*	black	*kukarma, duṣkarma*
iii) *śukla-kṛṣṇa karma*	white/black	are mixed actions with views and thoughts
iv) *aśukla-akṛṣṇa karma*	non-white & non-black	*niṣkāma karma*

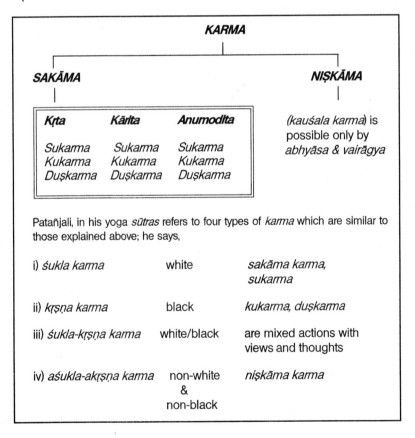

fear, attachment and possessiveness, and finally learn to surrender to the Lord.

In order to uniformly develop these qualities, we have to use first the *'bahiraṅga'* of man – the perceptible body – through the practice of *āsana-s,* to bring a rhythmic balance on the five elements of nature, *pṛthvi, āp, tej, vāyu, ākāśa* – earth, water, fire, air and ether.

As there is a backdrop on a stage, we need to keep the above points in mind as a backdrop when *āsana, prāṇāyāma, dhāraṇā or dhyāna* are practised.

Āsana and *prāṇāyāma* are inter-related, inter-connected, inter-supported, inter-dependent and inter-woven.As such, the *sādhaka* has to use his intellectual skill to commune with the various layers of the body which has their own ways on inter- communication to be felt by the self in his practices. . If *yama* and *niyama* together bring ethical purification and external cleanliness, *āsana* and *prāṇāyāma* bring internal cleanliness and sanctity. These two are *tapas* in yoga in order to eradicate the *tāpas* – the afflictions. *Tapas* also helps us to bear the onslaughts of the afflictions with tolerance.

To detect diabetes the sugar tolerance test is taken. Similarly, *tapas* is a tolerance test to see how much the body can bear pains and how much the mind can tolerate the afflictions.

In order to develop tolerance in the body and the mind, *āsana-s* are introduced so that we can bear the external onslaughts of stress and strain.

Many yoga masters and teachers ask one to do the *āsana-s* with ease, comfort and in a non-painful way. This is not only against the principle of yogic discipline but also it makes the *sādhaka* to live within the limits of the mind. By doing this in a non-painful way, the actual 'feel' of the *āsana-s* is neither felt nor expressed. As one limits the exploration of mind, the mind remains petty and small and therefore the practitioner restricts it, so that it does not move beyond its frontier. They loose the in-depth of precision in practice as attempts bring some effort and pain. This means that the subject matter of yoga is meant for the purification of body and inter-penetration of the mind. The mind must have the strength of will to bear the physical pain that comes in effortful effort.

Please note that no one can reach the peak in any profession without putting total effort bearing the pains and impediments that come in one's ways.

Those who do the *āsana-s* for the sake of health or to keep themselves fit or to maintain mobility, their practice just becomes a peripheral or external one as *bahiraṅga sādhanā*. These practitioner's bodies and minds are not soaked or immersed into the depth of *āsana*. Their practice of *āsana-s* has not made their bodies or minds to be juicy enough to pursue the in-depth to experience the finest effects of *āsana-s*. Therefore, their practice is superficial and dry.

Do not underestimate the value of *āsana-s.* One should know that even in *āsana, bahiraṅga* – external body, *antaraṅga* – inner body and *antarātma* – the innermost body are involved. *Bahiraṅga sādhanā* acts as the external or superficial body bringing firmness in the outer body. But what about the inner body with its contents namely, physiological, psychological, emotional, intellectual sheaths bringing steadiness of intelligence is *antaraṅga* and benevolence of spirit – *antarātma sādhanā?* We do not pay attention to all these various aspects of the inner body while performing the *āsana-s.* Often, we hear people saying that they remain active and light when they stretch the body even a bit in *āsana* practice. Even a rawest of a raw beginner experiences this state. Does not this feeling of being active and light sprout from *antaraṅga* though *sādhanā* is *bahiraṅga?*

To read the definition of *āsana* by Patañjali, requires intellectual intelligence. He says,

Sthira sukham āsanam II (*Y.S.,* II.46)

Sthira means firm, fixed, steadfast, enduring, lasting, still, serene, calm and composed. *Sukha* means delight, comfort, alleviation and bliss. The presentation of an *āsana* should be undisturbed, unperturbed and unruffled at all levels of body, mind and self.

Sthiratā points at *vṛtti-nivṛtti* – non-movements of thoughts and *sukhatā* points at *kleśa-nivṛtti* – freedom from afflictions. One may find it hard and difficult to grasp, but the truth is that when all sheaths and parts of man co-ordinate together while performing an *āsana,* then one experiences not only restraint of thoughts or the *vṛtti-s,* but also freedom from afflictions.

Āsana is a position where the practitioner works, co-ordinates and balances the *karmendriya-s* – organs of action, *jñānendriya-s* – senses of perception, the muscles, the ligaments, the tendons, the fibres, the sinews of the body as well as *manas* – mind, *ahaṁkāra* – ego, *buddhi* – intellect and *citta* – consciousness in unison, interweaving the gross physical body, the subtle mental body, and the causal – spiritual – body.

People ask why do you have to do so many *āsana-s?* Sit in one *āsana* and begin meditation. As said in the *Brahma Sūtra,*

Āsināt saṁbhavaḥ //

The Supreme or Ultimate Truth will be known by sitting in a posture for meditation – is a partial truth. One has to read its broad meaning.

Suppose we have to arrange a big gala programme, what do we do? We decide and say, "Let us sit together and discuss. Let us have a meeting. Let us work out the programme."

Exactly this kind of sitting is required if we are to know the Supreme. It is like a gala festival, a grand finale to know the Supreme. All preparations have to be done. All arrangements have to be made so that there is no room for confusion or doubt. All impediments have to be removed. Whatever extra precautions are needed have to be undertaken. For this reason, one has to practise many *āsana-s,* many *prāṇāyāma-s,* chalking out sequential programmes so that no fissures are left in the body, the mind and the self. *Āsana-s* are not meant to drain one's energy unnecessarily.

Even Vyāsa, in his commentary on the aphorism, *"sthira sukham āsanam",* has given a list of *āsana-s,* such as *Hastī-niṣadana, Uṣṭra-niṣadana, Krouñcha-niṣadana, Paryaṅkāsana, Vīrāsana* and so on. *Niṣadana* means dwelling in position. It means to dwell physically, morally, mentally, intellectually and spiritually, whether the *āsana* is a straight sitting position, a curved position, a reclining position or an inverted position. All these various *āsana-s* act as arrows pointing inwards guiding the practitioner to, "Peep in". As our minds are oscillating and vascillating either by *vṛtti-s* or *kleśa-s, āsana-s* and *prāṇāyāma-s* teach us this 'peeping in' or 'drawing in' process. *Sthira*–steadiness points to the restraint of *vṛtti-s* – *vṛtti nirodha* and *sukha* points to a contentment that is free from afflictions – *kleśa nivṛtti.*

Vyāsa would not have listed so many *āsana-s* if he wanted only one *āsana* to be done. He does not say, "Choose one amongst them". The variety of *āsana-s,* the variety of *prāṇāyāma-s* are done so that the clouds of doubt and confusion do not gather around the *manas* or *citta* in the form of diseases like breathlessness, illusion, false ideas, pride, wrong knowledge, attachment and aversion; but they are meant to take the *citta* towards calmness, serenity and single-pointed attention.

Āsana is for *snāyu-vṛtti nirodha*. *Snāyu* is not just the muscles, but the covering of the muscles, sinews, tendons, fibres, ligaments and cells. The *vṛtti-s* and the *kleśa-s* have to be eradicated from all parts so that the mind that is closer to the body is made to move deeper and deeper towards the core. Hence, the cells of the body have to vibrate in the *āsana-s* as a *japa* with the feel of coming closer to the *ātman*.

When Lord Hanumān found Sītā in Lankā, Rāma, along with his monkey army, had to march to Lankā. For that, they had to construct a bridge to cross the ocean. The engineer, called Neela, guided to build a bridge with stones on the ocean. As the stones were placed, they sank. Finally, Hanumān with the *nāma-japa* in his mouth, wrote the word 'Rāma' on the stones. To everyone's surprise they started floating. This is how the bridge was built from one end of the land to the other and the army crossed easily and safely to the other side. Similarly, in each *āsana* we have to write 'Rāma', or the name of God on each cell of the body to reach the *Ātmārāma* – the Soul. Otherwise we do not know which cell forms a fissure and creates illness in the body and restlessness in the mind. We have to purify and sanctify each cell to reach the Divine Self within.

Patañjali explains,

Prayatna śaithilya ananta samāpattibhyām // (*Y.S.,* II.47)

Perfection in an *āsana* is achieved when the effort to perform becomes effortless and makes the *sādhaka* to come closer to the infinite being. Thus, the practice of *āsana-s* as part of devotion becomes *antaraṅga sādhanā.* When the effort in *āsana* by the practitioner changes into an effortless state, the practice transforms his mind and consciousness to move closer towards his self. The eternal, ever-existing, non-perishing *Puruṣa* is *ananta. Ana* means never. It is a negative prefix and *anta* means end. Never-ending entity or infinite is *ananta,* the Soul. If the body, the cells and the mind gravitates towards the seer in the practice of *āsana-s,* then the practitioner not only experiences effortlessness in effort but also touches the infinite that is residing within in his practice. This is *antarātma sādhanā.*

Patañjali explains this state as *Tataḥ dvandvāḥ anabhighātaḥ* // (*Y.S.,* II.48)

By the precise perfection in the presentation of the *āsana-s,* the *sādhaka* remains undisturbed by dualities, because the blemishes on the *sthūla śarīra* – the gross body and *sūkśma śarīra* – the subtle body – are washed off. Tolerance of the body and mind increases. One gets physical equipoise, mental balance and spiritual benevolence as differentation between the body and mind and the mind and soul fades out on its own. By this, he experiences firm stability *sthira,* and freedom in the consciousness as *sukha.*

However, to follow the path of yoga, it is like walking on the edge of a razor blade. It is like standing on a cliff. If the wind is strong you can save yourself by moving to the safer side or fall on the otherside and get injured. To speak of a balanced mind towards pain and pleasure, loss and gain, shame and fame, defeat and victory is all right, but what about the state that arises where you feel like giving up the path itself? How many left off the practice and the quest for the soul? How many have been misguided? How many find the path difficult and adopt some simpler path? How many question, "Should I continue or discontinue?" These hidden inner dualities of the mind are subtler than the dualities such as honour and dishonour or fame and blame.

When the mind is caught in this state of duality, continue the practice of *āsana* judiciously, with discrimination and without losing will power and see what happens. My experience is that in my practice of *āsana* and *prāṇāyāma,* the contact of *prakṛti,* the body with the self is kept apart nullifying the guna-s to function. Precise practices of *āsana-s* and pr*āṇāyāma-s* saves the practitioner from a physical, moral, mental and spiritual fall. In addition to these, Patañjali says, in the *Vibhūti Pāda* that when the *sādhaka* gains perfection of the body it becomes the wealth of the body – *kāyasaṁpata. Kāya* – body – and *saṁpata* – wealth – is one of the effects of *āsana.*

What is this wealth of the body?

Rūpa lāvaṇya bala vajra saṁhananatvāni kāyasaṁpat // (*Y.S.*, III.45)

The aphorism explains four types of wealth. *Rūpa* – form, handsome and charming in shape and appearance, *lāvaṇya* – grace and beautiful, *bala* – strength and power, *vajrasaṁhanatva* – like a diamond – firm, compact, throwing different rays of light. In fact this four faceted wealth belongs not only to the body, but also to the mind, intelligence and soul. It gives strength to the body, form and shape to the mind, firmness and unwavering consciousness, intelligent understanding of the self and the grace in the soul. *Bala* of the *āsana* represents the body, *rūpa* of the *āsana* the mind, and *lāvaṇya* of the *āsana*, the Self.

Undoubtedly, when the body shows grace, beauty, strength and firmness, he or she becomes the centre of attraction. This may put him or her in a fix. Here, he or she may get caught up in dualities of the mind. To give up the *sādhanā* due to hardship is quite different to that of a downfall due to achievement or accomplishment. When one has acquired the wealth of the body, even then continuity is required. In these four types of wealth, the first two may have an aesthetic value, but the other two are meant to progress further in one's practice. So the *sādhaka* has to be careful as *rūpa* and *lāvaṇya* may not only allure him or her, but also may attract others to his or her beauty, charm and grace. This allurement is what Patañjali calls *avirati*, which means incontinence or lacking control (*yoga sūtra* I.30). I also advice you to refer to *sthānyupanimantraṇe saṅgasmayākaraṇaṁ punaraniṣṭa prasaṅgāt* // (Y.S., III.52) which means that he or she may be approached and enforced by such beings for undesirable connections and one may fall into this pit and pray. Hence, the *sādhaka* who has earned *bala,* the willpower and *vajrasaṁhananatva,* the compactness and brilliance of a diamond has to be careful in not falling into the pit of enticements but to continue *sādhanā* further in order to cleanse the intelligence further and further. Because, the intelligence which is the part of nature is the pinnacle of nature and it has to be in par with the pure intelligence of the soul. *sattva puruṣayoḥ śuddhi sāmye kaivalyam iti* // (*Y.S.,* III.56)

I may have diverted your attention from the main point, but I wanted to put a stress on the *dvandva-s* – the duality of mind – and how a downfall may come.

Each *āsana* has got its psychological and emotional aspects, apart from physical ones. Through the practice of *āsana-s,* we have to shape and mould our mind so that we know how to use it in the spur of the moment, when we are in a fix or in confusion.

As *vṛtti-s* are objective as well as subjective, the effect of *āsana-s* are also objective and subjective. The objective effects are like removing the dullness of the mind with *Śīrṣāsana,* or doing *Halāsana* for bringing high blood pressure down. Or you may do *Baddhakoṇāsana* to check the menstrual flow or quietness in sex organs, *Bharadvājāsana* to remove back pain, *Paśchimottanāsana* for calming the mind (see Table -18). But the subjective effects are realised only with ones own religiosity in practice with a devotional approach in *āsana-s.* The obstacles such as laziness, heedlessness and incontinence are likely to come in our way to distract us and allure us. If we know the subjective effect of *āsana-s,* we can overcome these obstacles. This is not an exaggeration and it has a vast scope for research. One need not be satisfied by doing the research on asthma, blood pressure and heart attacks as I have already carried them out long back. Patients have found great relief and many are saved from death. But here, what I say about the subjective effect is quite different. For this one has to have a continuous and faithful practice without any bias or doubt, without any prejudice. A correct practice with a pure mind and heart gives immeasurable, perhaps unfathomable benefit. When Patañjali says, *tataḥ dvandvāḥ anabhighātaḥ* – he is pointing at the subjective benefits.

The dualities have a direct connection with *triguṇa-s* – the three qualities, *sattva, rajas* and *tamas.* Evolution, called *prasava* and involution called *pratiprasava,* are dependent upon these three qualities. Evolution is a regular phenomenon which we witness constantly. But involution is a rare phenomenon which occurs only in a yogi who has reached the highest state of *samādhi.* For the realised yogi, *prakṛti* disappears. This disappearance, called *pratiprasava,* happens only at the end of effort. But the seed of *pratiprasava* is sown in the practice of *āsana-s.* He masters the *āsana-s* in order to get the subjective effect so that *dvandva* does not play any trick upon him. As he conquers the body and mind saving them from the onslaught of dualities, he gets the glimpse of *pratiprasava* though it is not yet a complete involution. This is the turning point in the practice of *āsana,* where the body, the mind and the self unite in a state of beatitude.

From this state the real *Īśvara praṇidhāna* begins. This is how the religiosity in the practice and devotional approach of *āsana-s* lead one to experience this undisturbed non-dual state. This is the meaning of *dvandvaḥ anabhighātaḥ* where the dualities between *prakṛti* and *puruṣa* come to an end and *Īśvara praṇidhāna* begins.

PRĀṆĀYĀMA

After mastery of the *āsana-s,* Patañjali guides and leads us towards *prāṇāyāma* for *prāṇa-vṛtti nirodha,that is,* restraint in the flow of energy. He expresses that there is a definite step between *āsana* and *prāṇāyāma* in order to attempt *prāṇāyāma.* He says, *"tasmin sati",* it means that unless one gains proficiency in the *āsana-s* one should not take to *prāṇāyāma. Prāṇāyāma* removes the defects as well as the obstruction in the flow of *prāṇa* – the vital energy. *Prāṇa* is wind, vital air. It also means power, aim and ambition in life. It points at willpower. *Āyāma* means stretch, expansion and extension. The expansion and extension of energy or the life-force and the development of willpower is *prāṇāyāma.*

Prāṇāyāma has four movements, *pūraka, recaka* and *kuṁbhaka.* That is inhalation, exhalation and retention. *Kuṁbhaka* is divided into *antara kuṁbhaka* – retention after inhalation and *bāhya kuṁbhaka* – retention after exhalation. The whole science of *prāṇāyāma* has developed several varieties or methods based on these four factors.

In the first aphorism on *prāṇāyāma,* Patañjali defines *prāṇāyāma.*

Tasmin sati śvāsa praśvāsayoḥ gativicchedaḥ prāṇāyāmaḥ // (*Y.S.,* II.49)

He says that *prāṇāyāma* is the regulation of the in-coming and out-going flow of the breath with retention.

He refers to the in-coming breath as *śvāsa* and the outgoing breath as *praśvāsa.* In the next aphorism, he does not use *śvāsa* and *praśvāsa,* but *'ābhyantara vṛtti'* and *'bāhya vṛtti'.*

At the end of each *śvāsa* and *praśvāsa,* he refers to *'gati viccheda'. Gati viccheda* means interruption in movement. This indicates *kuṁbhaka.* Here he gives just an introduction to *kuṁbhaka* and nothing more. In the succeeding *sūtra,* Patañjali refers to it as *staṁbha vṛtti.*

His words convey a very significant meaning when we notice and realise that the movements of our normal inhalation and exhalation take place only at the surface level. Sometimes the breath is felt in the nose, sometimes in the throat, in the chest or in the abdomen touching a bit here and a bit there. According to medical science, the normal breath is dependent upon the movement of the diaphragm but the touch of the normal breath always changes. One area works and the other rests. Though the breathing process is a continuous process there are interruptions and unfilled areas felt in the torso in its flow.

When we begin to observe the normal breath, we realise how the breath moves un-rhythmically, changing its place in the body by touching the nose or the throat at one time and the chest, the diaphragm or the abdomen at other times. We have to observe and learn to do inhalation and exhalation by removing these interrupted movements so that the breath moves rhythmically and spreads on the lungs evenly.

Hence Patañjali wants us to understand the depth of the respiratory system that is needed for the right method of *prāṇāyāma practices* through this aphorism, *tasmin sati śvāsa praśvāsayoḥ gativicchedaḥ prāṇāyāmaḥ* // (*Y.S.*, II.49)

One has to observe the motion and very action that are involved in the moods and modes of respiration so that we can build a certain discipline to practice it. This is the beginning of *prāṇāyāma*. A normal inhalation and a normal exhalation done with attention and absorption leads one automatically towards deep inhalation and deep exhalation filling the unfilled or empty places of the lungs. We call this *Ujjāyī Prāṇāyāma*, the beginning of the *prāṇāyāma* process.

This above practice of *prāṇāyāma* is a purely physical – *bahiraṅga prāṇāyāma,* which triggers alertness in the mind.

In *Samādhi Pāda, śvāsa praśvāsa* is listed as a distraction of the consciousness and in *Sādhana Pāda* as a construction for bringing restraint of the mind. This is because the moment the *citta* is distracted the *śvāsa praśvāsa* get affected. As the breath gets affected on account of the fluctuations of the *citta,* Patañjali advises this method of rhythmic *prāṇāyāma.*

He says, *Duḥkha daurmanasya aṅgamejayatva śvāsapraśvāsāḥ vikṣepa sahabhuvaḥ II* (*Y.S.,* I.31)

Sorrow, despair, unsteadiness of the body and irregular breathing distract the *citta.* Among these four, the first three, *duḥkha* – sorrow, *dauramanasya* – dejection or despair and *aṅgamejayatva* – unsteadiness or shakiness of the body, indicate the want of practice of *āsana-s* and the last one – *śvāsapraśvāsā* – indicates the want of practice of *prāṇāyāma.* If the *āsana* is not conquered, the dualities disturb us. Sorrow, despair and shakiness are the result of the unbearable onslaught of dualities and they reflect on the movements of the in-coming and out-going breaths.

I feel that Patañjali begins *prāṇāyāma* at the *Ujjāyī* level with the simple movement of breathing and then leads us towards the depths of *prāṇāyāma* with various *prāṇāyāma-s.* He says,

bāhya ābhyantara staṁbha vṛttiḥdeśa kāla saṁkhyābhiḥ paridṛṣṭaḥ dīrgha sūkṣmaḥ II (*Y.S.,* II.50)

Prāṇāyāma has three movements: prolonged fine inhalation, prolonged fine exhalation and prolonged stable retention. He then emphasises that these are to be attempted with precision according to duration and place.

In this *sūtra*, Patañjali refers to *śvāsa* – inhalation – as *ābhyantara vṛtti, praśvāsa* – exhalation – as *bāhya vṛtti* and retention as *staṁbha vṛtti. Staṁbha vṛtti* divides into two, *bāhya staṁbha vṛtti* and *ābhyantara staṁbha vṛtti. Bāhya staṁbha vṛtti* is exhalation/retention, and *ābhyantara staṁbha vṛtti* is inhalation/ retention.

The place of *śvāsa gati* and *praśvāsa gati* is now taken by *ābhyantara vṛtti* and *bāhya vṛtti* and the place of *gati viccheda* by *staṁbha vṛtti.*

There is a difference between the meaning of *gati* and *vṛtti. Gati* means a movement. This movement is vague. The *gati* or movement of *śvāsa* and *praśvāsa* is used in a general way for a beginner to grasp the subject. *Vṛtti* has a specific precise movement. That is why the movements of *citta* are specifically classified into five *vṛtti-s. Vṛtti* has a definite course of action, a definite course of movement, a definite direction.

The word *viccheda* indicates cutting as under. It is a process of piercing, cutting and dividing or cutting and diverting. In our normal breathing these kinds of *gati* are often experienced. The in-coming breath stops and suddenly changes its course of action and the exhalation begins. But the word *staṁbha vṛtti* indicates a definite course of stopping. *Staṁbha* means fixedness, stoppage restraint. It also means to get established firmly. If the retention or restraint of the breath is held properly, then, one can experience the moment with no movements in the consciousness or on the breath.

This disciplined movement of breath is regulated *deṣa*-wise. *Deśa* means place which indicates the constitution of the body. *Kāla* means duration which depends upon the circumstances that the body and mind undergo. *Saṁkhyā* means quality which indicates fineness and precision. Each of these, whether *deśa, kāla* or *saṁkhyā*, should be accompanied by prolongation and subtlety.

This aphorism clearly states that *prāṇāyāma* does not mean only breathing. The breath has to pervade the entire region of the body. The breath in the form of energy has to flow everywhere in the body. Whether it is inhalation or exhalation the breath should touch each and every nook and corner of the particular area we are dealing with when we lead the breath there. The energy needs to reach the remotest parts of the body with each and every breath. Hence, it should be long, strong, extensive, expansive and explicit. That is *dīrgha prāṇāyāma*.

When the breath is made soft, minute, fine, subtle and implicit, it is *sūkṣma prāṇāyāma*. *Dīrgha* is audible; *sūkṣma* is inaudible.

Dīrgha is expressive; *sūkṣma* is inexpressive. *Dīrgha* is active; *sūkṣma* is pensive. There is a deliberate regulation in this *prāṇāyāma,* whereas in *śvāsa-praśvāsa* there is no deliberate regulation.

Then, Patañjali comes to the ultimate end of *prāṇāyāma.*
bāhya ābhyantara viṣaya ākṣepī caturthaḥ // (*Y.S.,* II.51)

The fourth type of *prāṇāyāma* transcends the external and the internal *prāṇāyāma-s* and appear effortless and non-deliberate.

This fourth type of *prāṇāyāma* explained by Patañjali is where the breath is suspended without breathlessness. This retention of breath is not dependent on or connected with inhalation and exhalation. The retention is independent of breathing. It is an effortless and a non-deliberate retention.

Patañjali allots three aphorisms for this aspect of *prāṇāyāma.* These three involve *abhyāsa* and *vairāgya.*

The first two aphorisms explain the process or technique of inhalation, exhalation and two types of retention. Patañjali demands quality and quantity, duration and precision. All these have to be achieved only by *abhyāsa.* However, the last one is achieved by *vairāgya.* The retention, independent of inhalation and exhalation, can come only when the *citta* has patience and placidity. Unless the *citta* is free from taints and thoughts, this last type of *prāṇāyāma* cannot even be thought of. Therefore, unless there is *vairāgya,* this type of *prāṇāyāma* explained in the third *sūtra* on *prāṇāyāma,* is impossible to achieve. This *prāṇāyāma* is recognised as *kevala kuṁbhaka* by other yogi-s and yoga texts.

This state of suspended breath is an essential requirement for a *sādhaka* when he reaches *ekāgratā pariṇāma.* There is a *prāṇa sthairya* – stability in life force – and *citta sthairya* – stability of consciousness. As the *prāṇa* is restrained, the *citta* is restrained. When you first meet a great personality whom you respect or when you see something beautiful, the breath stops for a while on its own. Similarly, when *citta* comes face to face with the soul the breath stops atonce and ecstasy is experienced.

Patañjali clearly mentions the four types of *prāṇāyāma.* In the first three, he wants the disciplining of inhalations, exhalations and retentions so that they lead us towards a state where the support of the in-breath or the out-breath is not needed. However, this last one is a forerunner for *dhāraṇā, dhyāna* and *samādhi.*

We need all our efforts to master the *prāṇāyāma* explained in the first two *sūtra-s.* Varieties of *prāṇāyāma* are included in these two *sūtra-s.* It may be *Ujjāyī, Viloma, Anuloma, Pratiloma, Sūrya-bhedana, Candra-bhedana* or *Nāḍī-śodhana,* as explained in the other yoga text books. All these various types of *prāṇāyāma* along with *kuṁbhaka-s* and *bandha-s* are essential to train and tone the body, mind, senses, vital organs, intellect, ego and *citta* as well as the conscience so that they help us to face the soul fearlessly. Besides these, there are *sābīja* or *sālaṁba prāṇāyāma-s* and *nirbīja* or *nirālaṁba prāṇāyāma-s.* In *sābīja prāṇāyāma* the in-coming, out-going breath or restrained breath is supported and sanctified with *mantra-japa* – silent utterance of the *mantra.* In *nirbīja prāṇāyāma,* the *mantra* fades out on its own as the core gets totally involved in the *prāṇāyāma.*

Vṛtti prāṇāyāma relates to the duration of all the three factors; the inhalation, the exhalation and the retention. Patañjali refers to this as *kāla* and *saṁkhyā* of *sabīja prāṇāyāma.*

In all, there are eight types of *prāṇāyāma* introduced by Patañjali. The first one is *śvāsa praśvāsa gati* - or the movement of the in-coming and out-going breaths. The second one is *bāhya vṛtti* and *ābhyantara vṛtti* or the deep channelled inhalations and exhalations. The third one is *bāhya staṁbha vṛtti* and *ābhyantara staṁbha vṛtti* or the *bāhya kuṁbhaka* and *antara kuṁbhaka.* The fourth one is the same as the third one, but with attention on *deśa* – place-wise – and *kāla* – duration-wise. Here, all the four movements of *prāṇāyāma* are done with steady intelligence. The fifth one is *dīrgha prāṇāyāma* or the prolonged gross one. The sixth is *sūkṣma prāṇāyāma,* or the prolonged subtle one. The seventh is *saṁkhyā* – measured precision-wise. The eighth is *bāhya ābhyantara viṣayakśepi,* meaning beyond the inhalation and inhalation-retention and beyond exhalation and exhalation-retention.

The *Haṭhayoga Pradīpika* refers to *prāṇāyāma* as *kuṁbhaka* and explains *aṣṭa kuṁbhaka-s* – eight *prāṇāyāma-s* – namely

Nāḍī-śodhana, Sūrya-bhedana, Ujjāyī, Śitalī, Śitakāri, Bhrāmari, Bhastrikā, Plāvinī and *Mūrchhā.*

Patañjali shows the various ways to reach the finest and ultimate *prāṇāyāma,* while others take a leaf from Patañjali on *prāṇāyāma,* evolving and developing different types of *prāṇāyāma* and giving names to each *prāṇāyāma* (see table - 15).

In the *Sādhanā Pāda,* Patañjali explains *prāṇāyāma* in depth, thoughhe refers to it in the *Samādhi Pāda* and *Vibhūti Pāda* as well. While dealing in the*Samādhi Pāda on prāṇāyāma,* he says to utilise *prāṇāyāma* with passive retention after exhalation – *bāhya kuṁbhaka. Pracchardana vidhāraṇābhyāṁ vā prāṇasya II* (*Y.S.,* I.34)

to embellish, pacify and revitalise the *citta,* for *citta prasādanam. Citta prasādanam* means diffusing the *citta* gracefully and with delicacy.

In the *Vibhūti Pāda,* he says that when one conquers the *prāṇa-s* called *udāna, vyāna* and *samāna,* it leads towards the conquest of the elements and the senses – *bhūta jaya* and *indriya jaya.* With *prāṇajaya* – conquest of *prāṇa* – one becomes light, walk on water and levitate keeping oneself above swamps and thorns. The *sādhaka* glows like fire and increases the temperature of his body. He hears sound which normally the ears cannot receive. These all come under *prāṇa siddhi.*

Even Lord Krishna in the *Bhagavad Gītā* stresses the importance of *prāṇāyāma.* Lord Krishna explains the same first *prāṇāyāma* of what Patañjali says.

Prāṇāpānau samau kṛtvā nāsābhyantaracāriṇau II (*B.G.*, V.27)
Balance the out-going and in-coming breath that is moving within the nostrils; control yourself with the help of rhythmical quality of breath if you are intent on emancipation. *Samau kṛtvā* – means bringing rhythm and equilibrium. This is a *Samavṛtti Ujjāyī Prāṇāyāma.*

Next, Lord Krishna refers to *bāhya* and *antara kuṁbhaka-s.* He calls *prāṇāyāma* a sacred sacrifice. He indicates the *kuṁbhaka* or fourth type of *prāṇāyāma* that Patañjali explains, *"Bāhyābhyantaraviṣayākśepī".* He gives the list of sacrifices in the fourth chapter,and among them, one is *prāṇāyāma,*

Apāne juhvati prāṇam prāṇe 'pānam tathāpare I
prāṇāpāna gatī ruddhvā prāṇāyāma parāyaṇāḥ II (*B.G.*, IV.29)

Those who are devoted to *prāṇāyāma* restrain the course of the out-going and in-coming breath and pour the *prāṇa* into *apāna* and *apāna* into *pṛāṇa.* The chest is *prāṇasthāna* and the abdomen is *apānasthāna.* Pouring the exhalation into the abdomen means sacrificing *prāṇa* into *apāna.* Pouring inhalation into the chest means sacrificing *apāna* into *prāṇa.* This is how the *Prāṇāyāma Yajña* is performed. As in *yajna* – a sacrificing ritual – the ghee or clarified butter is poured into the fire, similarly, the yogi pours his vital breath or vital energy into the cosmic energy.

What is the effect of *prāṇāyāma?*

Prāṇāyāma is effective on all planes, the physical, mental, emotional intellectual and spiritual. Svātmārāma, in the *Haṭhayoga Pradipika* explains the benefit at the physical and physiological levels. Patañjali explains the benefit at the higher levels of consciousness.

Svātmārāma says that *prāṇāyāma* slims the body, brightens the face and manifests the inner sound called *nāda*. It clears the eyes, makes the body free from diseases, controls the seminal

Table 15. - *Prānāyāma*

PRĀṆĀYĀMA		
Patañjali	*Haṭhayoga Pradīpikā*	*Light on Prāṇāyāma*
Aṣṭa Prāṇāyāma	*Aṣṭa Kuṁbhaka*	
1. *śvāsa praśvāsa gati*	1. *sūrya bhedana*	1. *ujjāyi*
2. *bāhya ābhyantara vṛtti*	2. *ujjāyi*	2. *viloma*
3. *bāhya ābhyantara stambha vṛtti*	3. *śītali*	3. *bhrāmari*
4. *bāhya ābhyantara stambha vṛtti - a) deśa* – place-wise *b) kāla* – duration-wise	4. *śītakārī*	4. *mūrchhā*
5. *dīrgha*	5. *bhrāmari*	5. *plāvinī*
6. *sūkṣma*	6. *bhastrikā*	6. *bhastrikā*
7. *saṁkhyā* – measured precision-wise	7. *plāvinī*	7. *kapālabhāti*
8. *bāhya - ābhyantara - viṣayākṣepi*	8. *mūrchhā*	8. *śītali*
		9. *śītakārī*
		10. *anuloma*
		11. *patiloma*
		12. *sūrya-bhedana*
		13. *candra-bhedana*
		14. *nāḍī-śodhana*

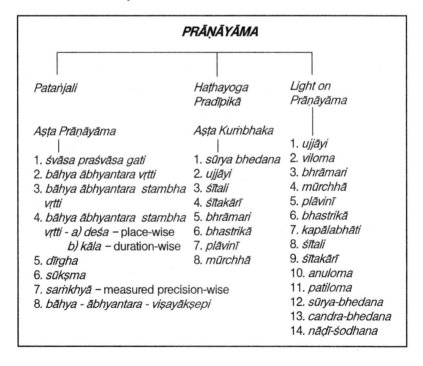

fluid, stimulates the digestive fire and purifies the *nāḍī-s.* Svātmārāma limits the benefits of *prāṇāyāma,* but explains the techniques in depth. Patañjali defines the whole of *prāṇāyāma* technique in three *sūtra-s,* which goes deeper than Svātmārāma's. He describes the benefits of *prāṇāyāma* in two *sūtra-s.* Svātmārāma explains objective benefits of *prāṇāyāma,* while Patañjali deals with the subjective benefits.

> Patañjali says, *Tataḥ kṣīyate prakāśa āvaraṇam //* (*Y.S.,* II.52) and *Dhāraṇāsu ca yogyatā manasaḥ //* (*Y.S.,* II.53)

Prāṇāyāma removes the veil covering the light of knowledge and heralds the dawn of wisdom and the mind also becomes fit for concentration.

Prāṇāyāma purifies and cleanses the mind and the *citta* making both a fit instrument for meditation. *Citta* has a capacity to acquire knowledge. But when it is veiled, it is hampered from getting that knowledge. The *citta* has three constituents – *sattva, rajas* and *tamas.* When the *citta* is clouded with *rajas* and perhaps more so with *tamas* then *sattva* is hidden. If the light is covered, it becomes dark. The sun is always throwing light energy but if you cover your eyes you don't see anything. Remove the cover on the eyes, then you begin to see. Night is not a defect of the sun. You can't blame the sun for it. Night is because the earth is rotating taking us away from the sun.

When the *sattva buddhi* faces the seer directly, there is complete illumination. Both face each other with purity, therefore, there is equanimity. Patañjali says,

Sattva puruṣayoḥ śuddhi sāmye kaivalyam iti // (*Y.S.,* III.56)

When the purity of nature's intelligence equals the purity of the intelligence of the Soul, the yogi reaches *Kaivalya.* This is perfection in yoga.

If there is a blank spot against the seer, darkness comes. Therefore, *sattva* shines partially. It is mixed with *vidyā* and *avidyā* – knowledge and ignorance, *śuci* and *aśuci* – purity and impurity, *sukha* and *duḥkha* – happiness and sorrow. When it is unveiled, there comes knowledge, purity, happiness, quietness and placidity. *Prāṇāyāma* is the first step for *sattva-śuddhi* because the veil of ignorance is removed and illumined intelligence begins to shine forth.

Prāṇāyāma unveils the *sattva.* The *sattva* which has an illuminating quality is covered by the darkness of *rajas* and *tamas.* *Prāṇāyāma* unveils *rajas* and *tamas* and the intelligence is illuminated by *sattva.* The illumined intelligence becomes fit to concentrate. The *tapas* of *prāṇāyāma* adds fuel to *jñānāgni,* the fire of knowledge.

The mind becomes a fit vehicle for *dhāraṇā* and *dhyāna.* The doubts, confusions and conflicts are like a smoke-screen covering the head and the heart. *Prāṇāyāma* clears the congestion in the head and the heart. This is *nāḍī-śuddhi.* Therefore, *prāṇāyāma* is called *prāṇa vṛtti nirodha.*

Unveiling the light of knowledge means clearing the head. That is *prakaśāvaraṇakṣaya.* Then the mind is clear and fit for concentration.

Dhāraṇāsu ca yogyatā manasaḥ II (*Y.S.,* II.53)

The intelligence of the heart and the intelligence of the head shine and march further in the path of yoga. In a way *prāṇāyāma* brings *aśuddhikṣaya* and *jñāna dīpti.As a matter of fact, the seat of the self is said to be in the head and the seat of Isvara or God is in the seat of the heart.Prāṇāyāma* unites the intelligence of the head or *jivatma* to the individual Soul or God that rests in the seat of consciousness or the centre of the heart. This is the true effect of *prāṇāyāma.*

Here, let us form a triangle. One side of a triangle is *tapas. Tapas, namely, yama, niyama, āsana* and *prāṇāyāma* leads further towards *svādhyāya. Pratyāhāra, dhāraṇā* and *dhyāna* come under the category of *svādhyāya,* building the other side of the triangle. *Svādhyāya* means to receive the instructions from a *guru* and then to build up from those instructions and afterwards to study independently. Though it is the *guru* who pours the knowledge, the *śiṣya* should be able to receive and understand that knowledge and wisdom. He should have a capacity for receptivity and adaptability to work on himself and digest this knowledge. The *śiṣya* has to be able to do a lot of 'homework' on his own that has been taught. This homework is considered as a part of *tapas*. Hence, *tapas* and *svādhyāya* go together.

Svādhyāya is divided into three types of *sādhanā* – *bahiraṅga*, *antaraṅga* and *antarātma*. The intensity in *svādhyāya* increases as one marches ahead in the path. *Svādhyāya* includes reading the scriptures, knowing their meaning and understanding the depth and intricacy of the subject. While performing the *āsana-s* and *prāṇāyāma-s*, one has to be able to sensitively verify differences in actions and implement adjustments. One has to watch the mind and its movements and keep the mind stable and quiet. These are all the characteristics of *svādhyāya*.

The study of scriptures and repetition of *mantra-s* is the *bahiraṅga sādhanā* of *svādhyāya*. *Svādhyāya sādhanā* is when one integrates thoughts and actions and evolves further from what one has learnt through the imprints stored deep in the heart; then it becomes *antaraṅga sādhanā*. *Svādhyāya* includes not only *bahiraṅga* and *antaraṅga sādhanā*, but the knowledge which comes directly from the core of the being. That is called *antarātma sādhanā* of *svādhyāya*. Here, introspection begins to bring an understanding of our strong and weak sides as well as our tendencies and attitudes as if we are reading our own book – the body, mind and self.

Patañjali says, *svādhyāyāt Iṣṭadevatā saṁprayogaḥ* II

(*Y.S.,* II.44) it means, that the study of the self helps one to communicate with one's desired deity. When you read the *Bhagavad Gītā,* you come closer to Lord Krishna. When you study the *Yoga Sūtra-s,* you come closer to Lord Patañjali. If you read the *Bible,* you come closer to Christ and understand Christianity. Similarly, learn to read your own body, its capacity and intelligence. Read your own mind, tendencies, behaviour, character, traits and trends. In this way if you continue, you begin to understand yourself – your own individual being. Your 'self' becomes your *Iṣṭa devatā. Iṣṭa* means desired, wished, liked. *Devatā* is deity. Whether one believes in other deities recognised by different religions or not; one certainly believes in oneself; therefore, the self – *ātman,* is *Iśṭa devatā* for the *sādhaka.* By knowing your self you move to know the *Puruṣa* – the Self – and then towards the *Puruṣa Viśeṣaḥ or Puruṣottama.* This is *Īśvara praṇidhāna,* the third side of the triangle.

This triangle of *tapas, svādhyāya* and *Īśvara praṇidhāna* can be equated with the other triangle explained in *Samādhi Pāda,*

Tasya vācakaḥ praṇavaḥ // (*Y.S.,* I.27) and

Tajjapaḥ tadarthbhāvanam // (*Y.S.,* I.28)

Here, the *japa* of the sacred syllable *auṁ* (God) becomes *tapas,* the foundation of the triangle. *Artha* as *svādhyāya* becomes one side of the triangle, bringing attention in the *sādhaka,* while *bhāvanam* as *Īśvara praṇidhāna* is the other side of the triangle, indicating the heartfelt realisation of the significance of God. *Tapas* is the path of *karma, svādhyāya* is the path of *jñāna, Iśvara praṇidhāna* is the path of *bhakti* (see Table 13).

PRATYĀHĀRA

Pratyāhāra, dhāraṇā and *dhyāna* as *svādhyāya* lead you towards *antarātma sādhanā*.

Pratyāhāra is *mano-vṛtti nirodha*. If *yama* and *niyama* chisel and regulate the movements of the mind through the *karmendriya-s* and *jñānendriya-s* – the organs of action and senses of perception then *pratyāhāra* directly works from the mind like a pneumatic tool for the mind to cut its outgoing habits by changing its direction to penetrate inwards towards the core. By this the mind is drawn towards spiritual morality and develops virtuosity through the *svādhyāya* of *pratyāhāra*. If the outgoing mind acquires knowledge of the external objects, *pratyāhāra* helps the mind to acquire knowledge of the self.

Pratyāhāra is a threshold between the first four and the last three aspects of yoga, namely, *yama, niyama, āsana, prāṇāyāma,* and *dhāraṇā, dhyāna, samādhi*. By following *yama* and *niyama,* mastering the intricacies in *āsana-s* and directing the movements of the breath, the *karmendriya-s, jñānendriya-s* and mind are trained to work in a disciplined and co-ordinated manner. By this co- ordinated disciplined manner the senses of perception and mind are drawn away from the external ideas and thoughts and are made to peep into the world of the body that is within. Though *pratyāhāra* is latent in the first four aspects, its study gets intensified in the next three aspects of yoga.

Pratyāhāra is a tableland for maintaining, sustaining and retaining what is gained through *yama, niyama, āsana* and *prāṇāyāma.* The cultivation of *pratyāhāra* is a *saṁskāra* – a culture on the mind – as senses often overpower and dictate to the mind. There will be a *vitarka bādhana* even in *pratyāhāra* and it has to be countered with *pratipakṣa bhāvanam.* Try to understand this. The mind does not like the discipline demanded by *yama* and *niyama* but likes to go out towards the pleasurable temptations. This naughty mind is controlled and channeled by following the disciplines of *yama* and *niyama*, while *āsana-s* and *prāṇāyāma-s* direct and guide the mind to move and know the inside world of the body. In other words, the practice of *āsana* and *prāṇāyāma* makes the mind ripe to follow *pratyāhāra.* Those who say that *āsana* and *prāṇāyāma* are external practices, I say that they do not know the depth nor the value of them. No *āsana* can be performed or done or experienced unless the mind co-operates and co-ordinates and reaches the various parts of the body. As exercise, you may stretch your gross and earthly muscles, like the hamstring or calf muscles, which may be considered as a muscle extension. But *āsana* is not just extending, flexing or bending of the muscles. It is aimed at correcting the positioning of the cells, the mind and the intelligence in order to transform the *bahiraṅga sādhanā* into *antaraṅga sādhanā.* This is the basic principle involved in the practice of *āsana* and *prāṇāyāma,* so that the mind of the *sādhaka* becomes intensely associated with and moves towards the *ānanda kāraṇa* and *ānanda kāraka asmitā* – the self, and then proceed to reach the *puruṣa* – the Self.

Similarly, *prāṇāyāma* is not just breathing exercise. One directs the energy inwards in *prāṇāyāma.* That is why Patañjali, while explaining the effect of *prāṇāyāma,* mentions that the mind becomes fit for concentration.

Dhāraṇāsu ca yogyatā manasaḥ II (*Y.S.,* II.53)

Why did he say that *prāṇāyāma* is not only an instrument to steady the mind but also the gateway for concentration? He could have said it in *pratyāhāra.* But he said it in the earlier step, because the actual process of internalisation begins in *prāṇāyāma.* That is how *pratyāhāra* evolves from *prāṇāyāma.*

Many while fishing, spend hours patiently waiting to catch a fish. *Prāṇāyāma* is a net thrown by the *sādhaka* who sits patiently to watch the senses and the mind to get caught in the *prāṇāyāmika* net. He does not know at what time they get caught. He does not know when the *pratyāhāra* begins in *prāṇāyāma.* He has to wait patiently and watch.

Pratyāhāra, undoubtedly is very difficult as one has to establish firmly of what the practitioner has learnt so far. Secondly, it is not an independent aspect. *Pratyāhāra* has to take the support of *āsana* and *prāṇāyāma* which discipline the organs of action, senses of perception and mind. Hence, the root of *pratyāhāra* is in *yama, niyama, āsana* and *prāṇāyāma. Pratyāhāra* has to be understood from the results that accrue from ethical discipline of *yama* and *niyama,* physical and physiological discipline by *āsana* and psycho-spiritual reaction through *prāṇāyāma*. It does not happen as easily as a fish gets caught in a net. The *sādhaka* cannot chase the senses and the mind, but has to learn to control them cautiously by attending to their moods and modes and rectifications. The practice of *āsana* and *prāṇāyāma* are done so that that they help to control the mind of the *sādhaka* to live in *pratyāhāra*. This makes us understand the depth of *sādhanā* in *āsana* and *prāṇāyāma*. *Pratyāhāra* begins in *āsana* and *prāṇāyāma* and reaches its maturity when these two aspects reach their culmination.

The mind, by nature, is fluctuating. It cannot remain silent and steady. You can never satisfy the mind and fulfil its wishes. The more you try to gratify the wants of the mind, they increase. The mind can shake the *buddhi*, *citta* and *viveka* – the intelligence, consciousness and conscience. Though these three are graded higher than the mind, the mind can shake them. Mind is *viṣayavatī* by nature. It always gets impregnated with the objects of enjoyment. Objects of attachment allure the mind and therefore in order to control the mind, one cannot be strict all the time. One needs to cajole, bribe and embellish it. If you cajole the mind without practising *yama*, *niyama*, *āsana* and *prāṇāyāma*, it swallows you. Therefore, with a background of the practice of the first four aspects, Patañjali asks us to cajole the mind at the right time. He says,

Viṣayavatī vā pravṛttiḥ utpannā manasaḥ sthiti nibandhanī II (*Y.S.*, I.35)

Contemplate on the object that helps to maintain steadiness of the mind.

This *sūtra* appears tricky, but at the same time gives a very clear signal. You cannot embrace the object when you are unable to contemplate. The mind, which flies like a butterfly from one object to another object, needs to be strictly controlled. There is a difference between a disciplined mind and an undisciplined mind in its choice of objects. The undisciplined mind chooses objects for its sensual satisfaction and pelf, whereas the disciplined mind chooses an object for its own good, the self for unalloyed contentment.

The *sādhaka* must always remember that the mind gets enticed towards the objects of attachment. It gets trapped very easily. Even the accomplished yogi cannot easily escape from the net of attachments.. The damsels come to allure him and he will be trapped unknowingly. Patañjali says not to invite such unwanted, undesirable events. At this stage of *antarātma sādhanā* of *pratyāhāra*, the aspirant requires stable, strong *svādhyāya* Or self-study. He requires intense self-study and self-examination to come out from these clutches successfully. When the mind and senses are controlled, the ego raises its hood up. It hisses. The heedlessness or *pramāda* – one of the obstacles – is created by the ego. The ego takes pride even in this controlled mind. Before the ego takes pride in it, the intelligence has to direct the energy of the mind towards concentration. That is why I say that *pratyāhāra* is very difficult to follow as it has to make the mind ripe to become virtuous so that the *sādhaka* is saved from his downfall.

This virtue is the jewel of the mind. The virtuous mind alone leads one towards *dhāraṇā*. The scattered mind is gathered and the gathered mind is made to concentrate.

Pratyāhāra is built, brick by brick through *yama, niyama, āsana* and *prāṇāyāma* and used in *dhāraṇa, dhyāna* and *samādhi*. The controlled mind that is gained in *pratyāhāra* is made to intensify its attention on a single thought as *dhāraṇā*. *Dhāraṇā* therefore, becomes *buddhi-vṛtti nirodha*. *Pratyāhāra* catches the thief- the mind, and *dhāraṇā* with *jñāna* and *buddhi* imprisons and rehabilitates it. If the mind as thief is captivated in *pratyāhāra*, then *dhāraṇā* sublimates and makes it subordinate to the intelligence. From then on the initiative is from the intelligence and not from the mind.

DHĀRAṆĀ

In *dhāraṇā*, *buddhi* is charged with *prajñā* – awareness – and made attentive. Intelligence has two faculties *prajñā* and *lakṣa* – awareness and attention. *Prajñā* is a special faculty of intelligence called wisdom. It comes with awareness. The intelligence uses this faculty of wisdom for *dhāraṇā*. The other faculty, *lakṣa* is the power of attention. It is this power that has to perceive, conceive and observe carefully.

In *dhāraṇā, lakṣa* and *prajñā* have to go hand in hand. Only then the focal point of attention is strengthened and enlightened.

Patañjali defines *dhāraṇā* in one *sūtra,*
Deśa bandhaḥ cittasya dhāraṇā II (*Y.S.,* III.1))
Dhāraṇā is the fixing of attention on one point or region.

In the *Sādhana Pāda,* Patañjali explained *yama, niyama, āsana, prāṇāyāma,* and *pratyāhāra* elaborately whereas in the *Vibhūti Pāda,* he defines *dhāraṇā, dhyāna* and *samādhi,* each separately in a single *sūtra.*

For *dhāraṇā,* one can say where to focus the attention but one cannot say how to focus the attention. These days, meditation classes are growing like weeds with people qualifying themselves as teachers of *dhyāna.* Often *satsaṅga* is considered as *dhyāna. Satsaṅga* is a group of people coming together for prayers. For *dhyāna,* one cannot assemble, one has to be alone. Actually *sat* means the real, the eternal and *saṅga* means to be in contact or in union with the real – the *Puruṣa.* Hence, *satsaṅga* means the union with the Self.

In the aphorism on *prāṇāyāma* and *dhāraṇā* Patañjali has used the word *deśa. Deśa* means place, region or a particular province. Vyāsa, while commenting on the aphorism on *dhāraṇā,* says that one can choose the place either inside the body or outside the body. It may be the navel, the heart, the centre of the brain or the forepart of the nose or tongue or it may be on any external object outside you.

There is a reason behind this option. A *sādhaka* does yoga either for *bhoga* – pleasures or joys, or *apavarga* – emancipation and liberation. These goals are poles apart. The accomplishments or the *siddhi-s* explained in the *Vibhūti Pāda* are going in two opposite directions. One is the objective accomplishments which are outside you. For instance, one understands the language of all living beings such as birds, animals, plants and so on. One is capable of understanding another's mind or entering into another's body. One is able to get the knowledge of planets, their orbital movements, the knowledge of stars, the Universe and visions of the accomplished ones – the *siddha-puruṣa-s.* The other is the subjective accomplishments; they are within you. These accomplishments are acquired by focusing within oneself. Vyāsa considers the subjective focusing points to be superior to the objective ones, since this internal focusing leads one directly towards the source, the Soul within. These could be navel, heart, *nāḍī-s,* throat, the gross elements and subtle qualities of the elements, the five *vāyu-s,* the *indriya-s,* the mind, the intelligence, the consciousness, the conscience and the *mūla prakṛti;* all existing in the body.

This internalisation of the focusing faculty has a direct connection with the first five aspects of *aṣṭāṅga yoga.* I want to invite your attention to what Patañjali says, *deśa bandhaḥ cittasya dhāraṇā* (*Y.S.,* III.1) fixing the consciousness on one point or region is concentration – *dhāraṇā*. I am quoting this since you are all doing *āsana-s*. People criticise *āsana-s* as physical yoga. Perhaps the reason for their criticism is that their practice is superficial. If they do just to limber, stretch and release the body, the experience will be limited. The *āsana* should be like a mirror. It has to reflect on your body, mind and intelligence for these to re-reflect in and out totally. The *āsana* is firm but at the same time transparent. If the *āsana* is opaque, there cannot be *prayatna śaithilya*. There cannot be effortlessness.

I ask you to watch every little thing. It may be just the bottom of your feet but you have to reach there you have to reach each toe the spacing of the toes, the mound of the soles, the pads of the heels, the metatarsals, ankles, outer edges, inner edges, arch and what not. I will not go into details. This write up is not a part of technique but it is a process of penetration. While you are doing the *āsana-s* as well as a point of concentration, a way of attention and observation is essentially needed for inner penetration. Are you or are you not focusing your attention and being aware of that attention wholly and soully?

Vyāsa says, "Choose the *deśa* from within, navel, heart, nose, tongue, forehead etc." Are these parts outside the body or inside the body? You do various *āsana-s* and you know how your concentration is drawn on a particular place as each *āsana* takes you to the different places of attention. Again in each *āsana*, you penetrate the attention varying the intensity of attention differently. In *āsana-s* like *Nāvāsana, Paśchimottānāsana* and *Pāśāsana,* (see table - 18), you reach the navel area but the depth and the intensity of penetration differs in each *āsana.* Similarly, this sensitivity is carried on in *prāṇāyāma,* where the outer body seems to be silent but the subtle senses like the intelligence and consciousness work differently to that of the *āsana-s.* In *dhāraṇā,* this contact is established further at a deeper level. That is how the eight aspects of yoga are inter-woven showing that they are not as separate entities but inter-related as a single entity.

While practising the *āsana,* one has to focus the total attention upon the inner body drawing the mind inwards and then sharpening the intelligence. A total effect of these put together is *dhyāna.* The *āsana* and *prāṇāyāma* brings the effect of *pratyāhāra* and with these three one gets transformed into *dhāraṇā.* A long uninterrupted length of time in *dhāraṇā* leads the *sādhaka* towards *dhyāna.* The fullness of *dhāraṇā* automatically changes into *dhyāna* in the practitioner.

The microscope reveals the details of the minutest cells. When you keep a leaf or a petal under the lens, it reveals the details. Even the transverse section of a leaf that is very small and thin reveals millions of cells. Similarly, while doing *āsana* and *prāṇāyāma,* you need to use the lens of awareness to see the required minutest part, so that it reveals the facts and gives you a chance to correct it. Patañjali says, *"paramāṇu paramamahattvāntaḥ asya vaśīkāraḥ* // (*Y.S.*, I.40) It means that mastery of contemplation brings the power to penetrate from the most infinitesimal particles to infinity.

Āsana, prāṇāyāma, pratyāhāra and *dhāraṇā*, function as a microscope. In *āsana* you see something gross. The same gross part becomes minute as you go on focusing. *Prāṇāyāma* reveals further detailed depths. *Pratyāhāra* intensifies one's attention to minutely watch the mind and *dhāraṇā* sharpens the intelligence of the mind by making it to focus attention on the tip of the nose or on the seat of the heart so that the inner mind becomes conducive to move towards the minutest part, the Self. As there are sacred places in the world, similarly, within the body, there are sacred areas. One has to trace and find out and establish the contact with the most sacred of all places in the body that is the Self.

When you have to watch the minutest cell under the microscope to find the defect in the cell, then you become keen to observe minutely. In the same way, yogic practice opens and broadens the intelligence to watch the minutest particles inside the body, mind and consciousness. This is *dhāraṇā*.

DHYĀNA

Dhyāna is skilfulness in spreading the intelligence evenly from the focal point as if all points are focal points. Hence, Patañjali says,

Tatra pratyaya ekatānatā dhyānam II (*Y.S.,* III.2)

Meditation means a steady, continuous flow of attention directed towards the same point or region.

When this attention flows continuously and uninterruptedly, it becomes *dhyāna*.

Ekatānatā is a key word in *dhyāna. Ekatānatā* is a technique, but inexpressible and inexplicable. The flow of attention is continuous and uninterrupted but at the same time it has to be even. There is no lassitude. The meditator should never get bored. As you renovate the house, you have to renovate your attention in *dhyāna.* Oil, when poured from one vessel to another vessel flows without breaks, without interruptions, similarly, the totality of the mind has to flow, charged with the same thought or object on which you are meditating. Hence, *ekatānatā* is not mere concentration but an un-interrupted flow of attention on the soul by the soul for the soul.

As we watch and observe minutely a cell under the microscope for various reasons, similarly, the aim or object can change in concentration. In case you watch the same cell continuously for the same reason, what happens? It may seem boring, meaningless and futile. This is exactly what happens in *dhyāna.* The *ekatānatā* is such that the aim does not change. The velocity of attention does not change. The potency of concentration does not change. The object does not change. The reason behind concentration or attention does not change. The intelligence does not put any question. The doubt does not arise. No sluggishness on the part of intelligence is felt. One has to keep one's awareness and attention not only sharp and one-pointed but all-pointed, and ever fresh dwelling in the abode of the Self. *tadā draṣṭuḥ svarūpe avasthānam* // (*Y.S.*, I.3) At that time the self or the seer dwells in its or in his own house with grandeur.

Therefore, *-dhyāna* is an *ahaṁkara-vṛtti-nirodha* – the restraint of the pride, ego and intellectual arrogance. The ego and intellectual arrogance not only become humble, but insignificant also. Neither the concentration nor the object of concentration becomes stale. *Prajñā* and *lakṣa*, the awareness and the attention, both remain fresh. Certainly *dhyāna* is not a mechanical practice but an electrifying practice.

Remember very well! More than the object of meditation, it is the meditation, the very act and procedure of meditation that is important as it does not change. Therefore, the object that one chooses should be not only conducive to meditation but also auspicious and spiritually uplifting since the aim of *dhyāna* is *samādhi*. When the object becomes the subject and the subject loses identity, *dhyāna* transforms into *samādhi*.

Patañjali says, "When there is *citta vikṣepa*, remove it with *citta prasādanam*". *Citta prasādanam* is closer to *dhyāna*. He says in one of the *sūtra-s*, *Yathābhimata dhyānāt vā* // (*Y.S.*, I.39)

Meditate on any desired object conducive to steadiness of consciousness.

The word *'abhimata'* indicates freedom of mind to choose. It is an open selection, a free selection. He leaves it to the *sādhaka*. "You choose", he says. It may appear democratic and secular, but the discipline and religiosity is hidden in it. If you choose the wrong object, you are caught and a downfall is certain.

What could be most pleasing to a real aspirant? What could be nearer and dearer to a yogi than that which he is seeking, the Self, the Soul? His whole life aspires for it. So what is this *'abhimata',* or 'according to one's own wish'? It is only the Soul and nothing else. If he were to say about the object for seekers the seer himself is an object. When the seeker has realised the seen he becomes the seer. The object has transformed into the subject. The seeker becomes the seer. *Dhyāna* transforms the tainted *asmitā* into pure unsullied *asmitā*.

Here, let me draw your attention to the various facets of *asmitā* as explained by Patañjali. One type is *kleśa kāraka asmitā* as ego which acts as an imposter to the Self. This *asmitā* is of *tāmasika* nature. The second type that springs out from the sense of 'I' is *rājasika* by nature as *nirmāṇa asmitā* or *pariṇāma asmitā*. It is a process of transformation to become better and better. It acts for progression. The third type of *asmitā* is from *saṁprajñāta ānanda kāraka asmitā* – a taintless state of *asmitā*. It is *sāttvika* by nature as it moves towards illumination.

Thus, the last three aspects of yoga, namely, *dhāranā, dhyāna* and *samādhi* takes the *sādhaka* to cross these three facets of *asmitā* – self, so that he touches the base of the individual self, the *Puruṣa* or the Self.

Coming back to *cittaprasādanam,* among the *sūtra-s* from I:33 to I:39, the last one is a subjective one. The rest are objective ones.

Yathābhimata dhyānāt vā II (*Y.S.,* I.39)

Meditate on any desired object conducive to steadiness of consciousness.

To diffuse the *citta* and to have its favourable disposition is *cittaprasādanam* (See *Y.S.,* I.33). You can cleanse and purify your emotions such as friendliness, compassion, joy and indifference or discipline the breath or discipline the mind or contemplate on a sorrowless state or effulgent light or feel the tranquil state by contemplating on great souls and sages. Or you can study and concentrate on wakeful, dreamy and sleepy states. All these are separate and different from the Soul. Therefore, they are all objective states of contemplation. I feel that Patañjali points out the Self as subjective in the 39th *sūtra.*

At two places, apart from the ones I mentioned above, Patañjali asks us to use *dhyāna* as a tool for the diffusion of *citta.* He refers to *dhyāna* as a tool for the attenuation of the afflictions. He says,

"The fluctuations of consciousness created by gross and subtle afflictions are to be silenced through meditation."

Dhyānaheyāḥ tadvṛttayaḥ // (*Y.S.*, II.11).

The afflictions whether gross or subtle, disturb the mind and create fluctuations. Yet these disturbances created by the afflictions have to be removed gradually and constantly. For this, *dhyāna* is the one remedy which minimises the afflictions, says Patañjali. Here the afflictions do not become the object for meditation. But the practice of meditation helps to reduce the onslaught of the afflictions. Patañjali says, *samādhi bhāvanārthaḥ kleśa tanūkaraṇārthaśca* // (*Y.S.*, II.2) It means that total contemplation absorption either removes afflictions or reduces their potencies or create strength to endure all afflictions with ease and comfort.

Meditation is meant to discipline the *citta*. It is not for gaining the *siddhi-s*. *Dhyāna* is explained as *bahiraṅga sādhanā* in *Yoga Sūtra* I.39 and II.11. *Dhyāna*, when leads one towards *samādhi*, it is *antaraṅga sādhanā*. Yet both *sūtra-s* are meant to discipline the *citta*. This is *citta vṛtti nirodhaḥ*.

If *tapas* is the first side of the triangle, *svādhyāya* is the second side of the triangle and *samādhi* is the third side of the triangle which completes the triangle. *Samādhi* is the result of *dhyāna* as *dhyāna* is the result of *dhāraṇā*.

SAMĀDHI

What is *Samādhi?*

Samādhi means total absorption. *Sama* means level, alike. *Adhi* means over and above. The seer is over and above the seen. Equalising the seen to the level of the seer is *samādhi.* It also means maintenance of the intelligence in a balanced state. *Dhi* is another word for *buddhi,* the intelligence. To maintain the *buddhi* in a state of equilibrium is *samādhi.*

Though *samādhi* can be explained at the intellectual level, it can only be experienced at the level of the heart. Patañjali says,

Samādhisiddhiḥ Īśvarapraṇidhānāt II (*Y.S.,* II.45)

Samādhi happens only by surrendering oneself to God. To reach *samādhi* the earthly bondage has to be released. An elevator does not take you up to the top storey of a skyscraper unless it leaves the ground floor. Similarly, unless the desires and attachments are left behind, you will not reach the *samādhi* storey. *Īśvara praṇidhāna* is a link between these two storeys; the bottom floor is called *vāsanā* – desire – and the top floor is called *samādhi.*

Īśvara is God and *praṇidhāna* means surrender. Though *praṇidhāna* is a single word it has a deep meaning. Surrender is not just a prostration. When you surrender yourself to someone you do not own anything at that time. A captive surrenders to the chief of the enemy. The chief of the enemy controls the captive. The captive loses his individuality.

Similarly, when there is *Īśvara praṇidhāna* we have to give ourselves totally to the Lord. The only difference is that we are not His captives, because we have surrendered ourselves willingly. *Īśvara* is not our enemy to use us or punish us. We have been made aware of what God is by Patañjali. He says,

Kleśa karma vipāka āśayaiḥ aparāmṛśṭaḥ puruśaviśeṣaḥ Īśvaraḥ II (*Y.S.*, I.24).

God, the Supreme Being is totally free from conflicts, totally free from afflictions, totally free from actions and their reactions as He is not *karma* bound. He does not hate anyone. He has no animosity. Neither does He punish. Any punishments or rewards are the effects of our own actions, our own makings, our own *karma-s.*

We perform rituals while worshipping God. We offer prayers, fruits or milk – *naivedyam* – and accept them as *prasādam.* This offering to the Lord has to be clean, pure and palatable. Krishna says, "Whatever you offer; offer it with a pure mind".

Coming back to the word 'surrender', there is an episode in the Rāmāyaṇa. Rāma, while searching for his wife Sītā, comes to the hut of an old lady, Śabarī who was a devotee of Rāma. She welcomes and offers him jujube fruits. While offering she first tastes each fruit herself and then offers them to Rāma. This, she does purely out of love, with a pure heart so that Rāma does not taste half-ripe, rotten or spoiled fruit.

From Śabarī, we have to learn to offer ourselves to the Lord with purity in our body, organs, senses, mind, intelligence, *citta* and conscience. *Samādhi* is the state where everything is clean, everything is pure. Therefore, there is a total surrender.

STAGES OF *SAMĀDHI*

Patañjali has given several stages of *samādhi.* There is a difference of opinion amongst scholars about these stages. I don't want to enter into those arguments here.

However, let me point out one fact, that Patañjali clarifies each step of *samādhi.* His explanation is crystal clear. Therefore, it is for the *sādhaka* to analyse each step to reach the ultimate goal. Patañjali deals with each step as explained in Table 16.

On the aspect of *āsana* and *prāṇāyāma,* people question why should one do so many types of *āsana-s* and *prāṇāyāma-s?* But nobody questions why Patañjali has given so many stages of *samādhi.* All the aspirants and practitioners of yoga should know that the different stages of *samādhi* are explained in order to master the *citta* and bring it on par with the purity of the Self. Similarly, so many *āsana-s* and *prāṇāyāma-s* are required to bring the cells of the body, the sinews of the body and the mind on par with the soul.

Patañjali defines *samādhi* in one aphorism,

Tadeva arthamātranirbhāsaṁ svarūpaśūnyam iva samādhiḥ // (*Y.S.*, III.3).

When the object of meditation engulfs the meditator, appearing as the subject, self-awareness is lost. This is *samādhi*.

The meditator loses his own identity. All this time, the meditator as a seeker identified himself with all the paraphernalia such as body, organs of action, senses of perception, mind, intelligence, ego and so forth. But now that he is pure, he is totally with the self without the feel of this paraphernalia. He is the soul.

Patañjali is not asking his followers to reach the level of the soul straight away. His *aṣṭāṅga yoga* is like an elevator that takes us upwards, crossing each storey. You cannot explain to a school going child higher subjects taught at university level. In the same way a pupil has to build up stage by stage and step by step to come to the level of *samādhi*. As such, it cannot be explained. Whatever is explained will be just verbosity leading towards hair-splitting arguments. Therefore, Patañjali waits. He asks the *sādhaka* to know each of the coverings that are hiding the Self.

Samādhi is mainly the *jñāna* of *antaḥkaraṇa* or conscience, known as virtuous sense – *dharmendriya*. As we sharpen a pencil to get its end sharp, in *dhyāna* the extreme end point of *buddhi* has to get sharpened to merge in the *antaḥkaraṇa*.

Table 16. - Classification of *Samādhi*

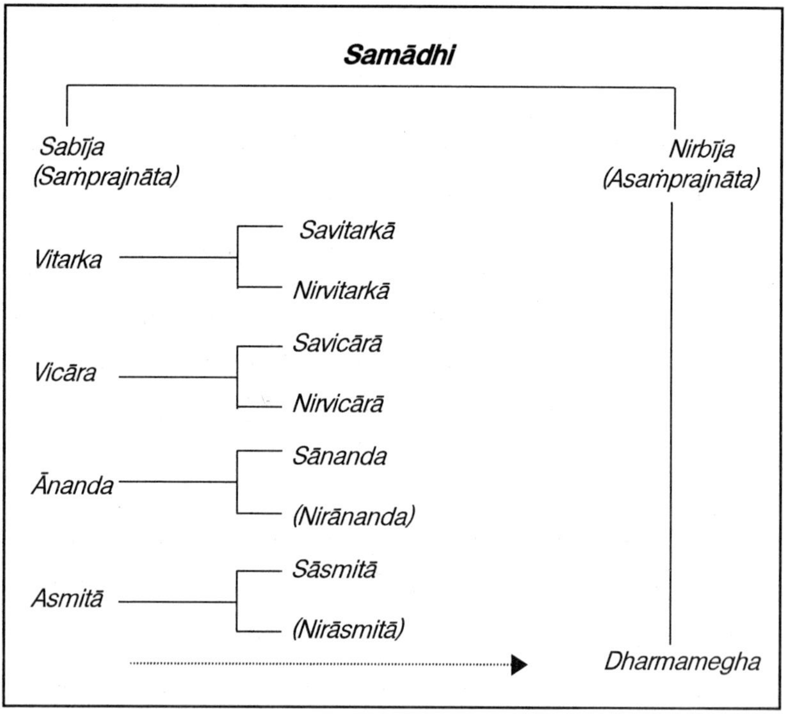
Samādhi
Sabīja
(Saṁprajnāta)
Nirbīja
(Asaṁprajnāta)
Vitarka
Savitarkā
Nirvitarkā
Vicāra
Savicārā
Nirvicārā
Ānanda
Sānanda
(Nirānanda)
Asmitā
Sāsmitā
(Nirāsmitā)
Dharmamegha

In *samādhi*, the thoughts are trimmed and the modifications of *citta* fade away. There is *ekatānatā* of the *citta*. At this point of culmination, the *citta* is full with one single thought and that is the soul. There is no other thought. *Citta* faces the soul. *Samādhi* is seeing the soul, face to face. This brings the *antaḥkaraṇa-vṛtti nirodha*.

Samādhi, like *prāṇāyāma* has two types – *sabīja samādhi* and *nirbīja samādhi*. Vyāsa names *sabjīa* as *saṁprajñāta samādhi* and *nīrbīja saṃādhi* as *asaṁprajñāta samādhi*. However, Patañjali has not used the word *asaṁprajñāta samādhi.* He mentions only *nīrbīja samādhi.*

Sabjīa means 'auspicious seed'. As the tree grows from the seed the intelligence ripens from the seed *samādhi.* That is *sabīja samādhi. Sabīja samādhi* is with content. Whenever there is an object for the *citta* to reach the *samādhi* state, it is *sabīja samādhi.* In *dhāraṇā,* the choice is left to the *sādhaka* to sow the seed. It could be either external or internal. In *samādhi,* the *sādhaka* uses the object chosen in *dhāraṇā* and proceeds to sharpen the intelligence step by step, stage by stage. These steps are *savitarkā, nirvitarkā, savicārā, nirvicārā, sānanda* and *sāsmitā.* Some also add *nirānanda and nirāsmitā* (see table - 16).

Sabīja is considered *bahiraṅga* to *nīrbīja samādhi. Nirbīja* means 'without seed'. It is a state of 'seedless' *samādhi.* In *sabīja samādhi* there is an access. In *nirbīja samādhi* there is no access. If you understand *sabīja samādhi* it will be easier for you to know why the other one is called *nirbīja samādhi.*

By the practice of the first seven aspects of yoga, from the gross level point of view *tasya saptadhā prāntabhūmiḥ prajñā II* (*Y.S.,* II.27) which means that through un-interrupted discriminative attention, the *sādhaka* trims a) his body, b) organs of action, c) senses of perception, d) mind, e) intelligence, f) ego and g) consciousness. The intelligence of all these evolutes are at a gross level. In *samādhi* they are transformed to a subtle level.

The *sādhaka* becomes sure about his own world. The desires are lessened. The contact with the outer world is lessened. The ripples of the mind – the waves of *citta* – are lessened and now the *citta* surfaces without any ripples – clean and clear.

When *citta* is clear of thoughts, it becomes transparent. It becomes crystal clear. As a flawless crystal reflects any colour without any mixture, *citta,* which is pure and untainted, reflects the object of thought clearly. The object of thought could be an external one it could be the *citta* itself and it could also be the seer.

The *samādhi* is also referred to as *samāpatti. Samāpatti* means coming together for transformation. Amongst the object of thought, the *citta* and the seer, there is an encounter that leads one towards clarity. *Samādhi* means a *sādhanā* or a practice to reach the state of clarity.

We name each *āsana.* These names are meaningful. They convey the shape, the direction or the technique. Therefore, we say *Sālaṁba Śīrṣāsana* for the posture in which we stand on the head, *UtthitaTrikoṇāsana* for the posture in which the triangle is formed as a right angle triangle. It also means the association and union of body, intelligence and self as one.

Logical intelligence leads one further to see the truth in the facts. Here, thinking is further deepened. From the *vitarka samāpatti* – logical deliberation – *citta* changes its posture to *vicāra samāpatti.* From deliberation, the *sādhaka* focuses on reasoning.

In deliberation there are many loose ends. *Vicāra samāpatti* gathers the loose ends and if necessary cuts the loose ends.

Vicāra means reasoning. It also means differentiating the knowledge. It has again two branches, *savicārā* and *nirvicārā*, reasoning and non-reasoning. The beginning of reasoning is *savicārā* and when it arrives at a satisfactory end it is *nirvicārā*. In *savicārā* there is a continuous investigation and reflection, whereas

Table 17. - The Depth of *Sādhanā*

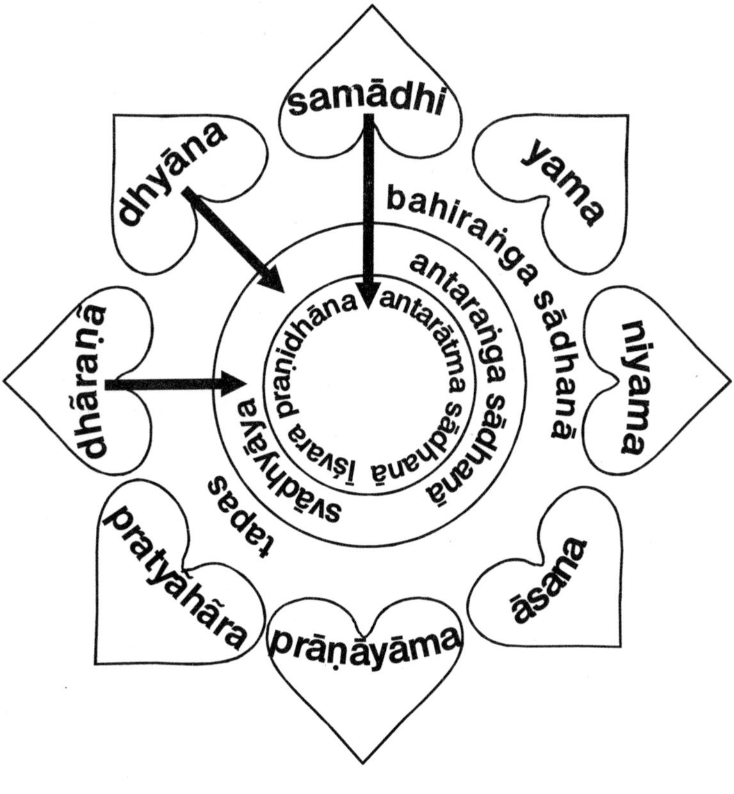

in *nirvicārā*, the investigation comes to a positive end or conclusion. All these four, the *savitarkā* and *nirvitarkā* as well as the *savicārā* and *nirvicārā* show the process of thinking, analysing, reasoning and establishing the fact. If the object of thought is gross, then it does not exert our brain much. But, if the object of thought is very subtle we say, "Oh! wait, let me think." Similarly, to think of the Soul, to think of God, is subtle thinking. Logical and analytical thinking does not help much at this point. But *savicārā* leads towards subtle thinking on subtle matters. From here begins the true *samādhi*.

Here, the *buddhi* feels an inner contentment. This contentment of *buddhi* after its hard work is recognised as *adhyātma prasāda*. Patañjali says, *"nirvicāra vaiśāradye adhyātmaprasādaḥ ll"*, (*Y.S.*, I.47). meaning, from proficiency in *nirvicārā samāpatti* comes purity. *Sattva* or luminosity flows undisturbed, kindling the spiritual light of the Self. There comes the purity and serenity in *citta*. The *citta* that covers the soul becomes clear. When the clouds covering the sun move away, the sun shines brilliantly. In the same way when the coverings of the soul in the form of afflictions, fluctuations and impediments are removed, the soul shines brillianty in its own glory.

Compare the state of *prayatna śaithilya* or effortless state in *āsana* to this state of *adhyātma prasāda* or grace of the soul. Here, it is nothing but the effortless state of the *citta*. What we achieve by *āsana* in a gross level, is achieved in *samādhi* in a subtle form.

This effortless state or this serenity of contentment is not superimposed on *citta*. It is an achievement of *citta* which leads towards *ānanda samāpatti*. *Ānanda* means un-alloyed and untainted bliss. When the intelligence is contented with its investigation, there comes the feeling of fulfilment. The bliss that is experienced through fulfilment is called *sānanda*. The proficiency in *nirvicārā samāpatti* is purity. Here, both memory and intelligence are cleansed. This leads towards that un-alloyed and untainted bliss. However, the 'I' principle for which we use the terminology of ego, remains to shadow the intelligence. The *citta* reflects the 'I' principle at this stage. This 'I' principle – *asmitā samāpatti* – needs to be submerged into the unmanifested form of *prakṛti*, called *alinga* or without any marks. It is a noumenal state. Once the 'I' ness of ours, the very mark of our existence is submerged in the unmanifested *prakṛti*, then begins the journey towards *nirbīja samādhi*.

Savitarkā and *nirvitarkā samādhi* belongs to the function of the brain. *Savicārā* and *nirvicārā* belongs to the realm of mind. *Sānanda samādhi* belongs to the realm of matured intelligence and *asmitā* belongs to the realm of the 'I' principle. In *nirbīja samādhi*, this 'I' principle evaporates and nothing exists except the soul. Patañjali explains it as, *"tadā draṣṭuḥ svarūpe avasthānam II"*, (*Y.S.*, I.3) meaning, then the soul dwells in its own true splendour.

Here, the triangle of *tapas*, *svādhyāya* and *Īśvara praṇidhāna* is complete. However, between *sabīja* and *nirbīja* there is a vast space, like the Pacific Ocean. In *āsana*, the dualities between *prakṛti* and *puruṣa* or nature and soul end only after the effortless stage – *prayatna śaithilya* – and in complete surrender – *ananta samāpatti* takes place. It means that the dualities do not end immediately. There is a time gap between *ananta samāpatti* and the non-dual state of *citta*.

Similarly, a gap remains between *sabīja* and *nirbīja samādhi*. It is really surprising that Patañjali uses the word *ananta samāpatti* in the context of *āsana*. *Ananta* means endless or eternal. *Samāpatti* means to bring all those forces together for transformation. This has the effect of halting the onslaught of dualities that gets created by the senses as phenomenal knowledge. The dualities come, but they are kept in a state of suspension. Hence, they do not affect the *sādhaka*.

The *siddhi-s*, being the fruits of *samādhi* act as obstacles in *samādhi*. The onslaughts of *siddhi-s* do come. If the *sādhaka* chooses the *siddhi-s* in order to enjoy them, he can do that because the *asmitā* tempts him to enjoy the *siddhi-s*. Or, the *sādhaka* may rest for a while in a highly evolved state of intelligence which is called *virāma pratyaya*. *Virāma* means rest or repose.

In a big city like Mumbai, you come to a circle where several roads meet. As a new comer to the city, you get confused and lost. You don't know which way to go. The state between *sabīja* and *nirbīja samādhi* is exactly the same. The intelligence gets diverted. The *sādhaka* becomes puzzled. It is like a spiritual plateau.

One may rest there or run after *siddhi-s* or one may proceed for further progress of transformation to trace *nirbīja samādhi.* However, the obstacles play even at this stage. I said this in the beginning, now I remind you here. Those who prefer to choose the road of the *siddhi-s* – the accomplishments – will enjoy these powers. But, Patañjali says,

Te samādhau upasargāḥ vyutthāne siddhayaḥ // (*Y.S.*, III.38).

He is saying that these attainments are impediments to *samādhi,* although they are powers in active life.

These achievements are not meant for showmanship to the external world. They are meant for the *sādhaka* to judge how far he has progressed. If one indulges in these accomplishments, they will divert him away from *nirbīja samādhi.*

At this stage of accomplishment, what one requires is *vairāgya,* desirelessness, indifference towards the *siddhi-s* and friendship with *kaivalya.*

The *siddhi-s* will make you the Lord of this world. You can show supremacy with all the manifestations. You will know everything, since there is a *pradhāna jaya* or the conquest of the first principle of nature. *Mūla prakṛti* tempts you towards accomplishments. It says, "Look! You are the master. You are the monarch". But the *sādhaka* should be cautious. If *prakṛti* says that the *siddha puruṣa* is the king, then the *prakṛti* as a queen, influences the *siddha puruṣa* back towards temptations to be caught again in afflictions. Here, Patañjali cautions the *siddha puruṣa* to be careful.

But know very well that we have to become *kṛtarthan-s* by reaching the end aim of life, namely emancipation. As I said earlier, *prakṛti* – the seen – disappears for him whose purpose has been fulfilled. The *prakṛti* says "goodbye" to the seer. If it does not say, "goodbye", then know that there is something waiting for you.

Sthānyupanimantraṇe saṅgasmayākaraṇaṁ
punaraniṣṭa prasaṅgāt // (*Y.S.*, III.52)

When approached by celestial beings, there should be neither attachment nor surprise as undesirable connections create unnecessary or unwanted problems again. At this juncture Patañjali, like a parent protecting his children, warns, "Do not get caught. Do not get enchanted. Do not get attached. Do not show any surprise. Do not wonder yourself, otherwise you have to wander again. Do not end up in any undesirable connection otherwise you will be disconnected from the ultimate goal." What a caution! How much care! How much love he shows towards his followers and towards his devotees! *Hānam eṣāṁ kleśavat uktam*(*Y.S.*, IV.28)As a raw beginner strives to be free from afflections, the *yoga siddhan* must not be caught in these *siddhi-s*. Otherwise he has to strive again from the start to reach the level that he has touched and lost.

If the *sādhaka* remains on the spiritual plateau, then he is in trouble. He gets caught in the web of bodiless feeling. He will be a *videhin* – without a body. He will end up as a *prakṛtilayin* – getting absorbed in the elements of *prakṛti*, ending up in an incomplete quest.

Others who do not get caught in this 'half-hanging' state, such as the state of *videhin* or the state of *prakṛtilayin*, will be at a hang-over state.

In the same way there is a transitional state between *sabīja* and *nirbīja samādhi*. Since, the feeling of 'I' is not lost and since there is not a total surrenderance, the *sādhaka* lands on a spiritual plateau. This state, Patañjali explains as different and separate from both *sabīja* and *nirbīja samādhi*. One may feel at the end of the journey. But at this stage there will not be progress, a fall is certain. "So do not rest there, proceed further", warns Patañjali. Read *śraddhā vīrya smṛti samādhiprajñā pūrvakaḥ itareṣām II* (*Y.S.*, I.20) – With faith, with strong memory, with valour, vigour, willpower and strength, and above all, "with a balanced intellect charged with awareness". This is *samādhi prajñā*.

People ask how many days will it take to learn *āsana-s?* How many days will it take to learn *prāṇāyāma?* They count the course in terms of days. Even months are too long for them. Here I am very much criticised because I have not charted out any course in periods of time. But here, Patañjali clearly mentions that these kinds of plateaus will be seen at each and every level. If the practitioner stops at these levels, he is lost on these plateaus.

Well! When the *sādhaka* proceeds on the path of *nirbīja samādhi,* some of the *saṁskāra-s* arise and come in the way. Though the *sādhaka* endeavours to wash off the *saṁskāra-s* – the old impressions – the *saṁskāra-s*peep again, creating perhaps small fissures or pain in the *citta.* At this stage the *citta* becomes *chidra citta. Chidra* means fissure. You have seen the ant, a small creature paving its path through a small hole in a thickly cemented wall. Similarly, even if *citta* is cleared, the *saṁskāra,* which was forgotten or unknown may surface. When that too is conquered there comes *dharmamegha samādhi* – the ultimate end, the Everest – the highest peak of the mountain of yoga. *prasaṁkhyāne api akusīdasya sarvathā vivekakhyāteḥ dharmameghaḥ samādhiḥ* //(*Y.S.,* IV.29) It means the *sādhaka* who shows no interest even in the highest state of evolution in involution, in him pours the stream of virtue.

Then there is *duḥkha-vṛtti nirodha,* there is *saṁskāra-vṛtti nirodha,* there is *kleśakarma nivṛtti,* there is *citta-vṛtti nirodha,* there is *guṇapariṇāma krama samāpti.*

Thus the tree of yoga with its eight branches helps us to unite all the facets in us from the elements of nature to the Soul to get free from all *tāpa-s* or afflictions through *sādhanā.* As the essence of the tree is in the fruit, the essence of *yoga sādhanā* is in *samādhi* and in *kaivalya(aloneness with fullness).*

The *prakṛti* says "goodbye". The seer says "hello!" The seer dwells in his own true splendour.

List of Yoga *Sūtras* of *Patañjali* referred to by B.K.S. Iyengar.

1) *Aparigrahasthairye janmakathaṁtā saṁbodhaḥ* – II:39
2) *Atha Yogānuśāsanam* – I:1
3) *Bāhya ābhyantara stambha vṛttiḥ deśa kāla saṁkhyābhiḥ paridṛṣṭaḥ dīrgha sūkṣmaḥ* - II:50
4) *Bāhya ābhyantara viṣaya ākṣepī caturthaḥ,* – II:51
5) *Deśa bandhaḥ cittasya dhāraṇā* – III:1
6) *Dhāraṇāsu ca yogyatā manasaḥ* – II:53
7) *Draṣṭṛdṛśyayoḥ saṁyogaḥ heyahetuḥ* – II:17
8) *Duḥkha daurmanasya aṅgamejayatva śvāsapraśvāsāḥ vikṣepa sahabhuvaḥ* – I:31
9) *Heyaṁ duḥkham anāgatam* – II:16
10) *Kleśa karma vipāka āśayaiḥ aparāmṛṣṭaḥ puruṣaviśeṣaḥ Īśvaraḥ* – I:24
11) *Kṛtārthaṁ prati naṣṭam api anaṣṭaṁ tadanya sādhāraṇatvāt* – II:22
12) *Nirvicāra vaiśāradye adhyātmaprasādaḥ* – I:47
13) *Pracchardana vidhāraṇābhyāṁ vā prāṇasya* – I:34
14) *Prayatna śaithilya ananta samāpattibhyām* – II:47
15) *Rūpa lāvaṇya bala vajra saṁhananatvāni kāyasaṁpat* – III:47
16) *Samādhisiddhiḥ Īśvarapraṇidhānāt* – II:45
17) *Sattva puruṣayoḥ śuddhi sāmye kaivalyam iti* – III:56
18) *Sattvaśuddhi saumanasya aikāgrya indriyajaya ātmadarśana yogyatvāni ca* – II:41
19) *Sa tu dīrghakāla nairantarya satkāra āsevitaḥ dṛḍhabhūmiḥ* – I:14
20) *Śaucāt svāṅgajugupsā paraiḥ asaṁsargaḥ* – II:40

21) *Sthānyupanimantraṇe saṅgasmayākaraṇaṁ punaraniṣṭa prasaṅgāt* – III:52
22) *Sthira sukham āsanam* – II:46
23) *Svādhyāyāt Iṣṭadevatā saṁprayogaḥ* – II:44
24) *Svasvāmiśaktyoḥ svarūpopalabdhihetuḥ saṁyogaḥ* – II:23
25) *Tadā draṣṭuḥ svarūpe avasthānam* – I:3
26) *Tadeva arthamātranirbhāsaṁ svarūpaśūnyam iva samādhiḥ* – III:3
27) *Tajjapaḥ tadarthbhāvanam* – I:28
28) *Tasmin sati śvāsa praśvāsayoḥ gativicchedaḥ prāṇāyāmaḥ* – II:49
29) *tasya vācakaḥ praṇavaḥ* – I:27
30) *Tataḥ kṣīyate prakāśa āvaraṇam* – II:52
31) *Tataḥ dvandvāḥ anabhighātaḥ* – II:48
32) *Tatra pratyaya ekatānatā dhyānam* – III:2
33) *Te samādhau upasargāḥ vyutthāne siddhayaḥ* – III:38
34) *Viṣayavatī vā pravṛttiḥ utpannā manasaḥ sthiti nibandhanī* – I:35
35) *Vátti sārūpyam itaratra* – I:4
36) *Vyādhi styāna saṁśaya pramāda ālasya avirati bhrāntidarśana alabdhabhūmikatva anavasthitatvāni* – I:30
37) *Yama niyama āsana prāṇāyāma pratyāhāra dhāraṇā dhyāna samādhayaḥ aṣṭau aṅgāni* – II:29
38) *Yathābhimata dhyānāt vā* – I:39
39) *Yogāṅgānuṣṭhānāt aśuddhikṣaye jñānadīptiḥ āvivekakhyāteḥ* –II:28
40) *Yogaḥ citta vṛtti nirodhaḥ* – I:2